# RISKY BUSINESS

*My Adventures with Jesus
in Many Languages*

# RISKY BUSINESS

*My Adventures with Jesus
in Many Languages*

PAULINE STABLEFORD

**Ambassador International**
Greenville, South Carolina • Belfast, Northern Ireland

RISKY BUSINESS
© Copyright 2007 Pauline Stableford

ISBN  978-1-84030-178-6

Ambassador Publications
a division of
Ambassador Productions Ltd.
Providence House
Ardenlee Street,
Belfast,
BT6 8QJ
Northern Ireland
www.ambassador-productions.com

Emerald House
427 Wade Hampton Blvd.
Greenville
SC 29609, USA
www.emeraldhouse.com

# CONTENTS

# FOREWORD

In the account of the missionary journeys of the Apostle Paul the term is used "in journeyings often" (2 Cor 11 v 26). I am tempted to use the same expression for Pauline's ministry in the different countries mentioned in the manuscript, which I have read with much interest.

I made visits in an administrative and preaching capacity to the Scandinavian countries during her time there, namely Finland and Sweden. I had visited Denmark, Norway and the Faroe Islands earlier. The difference in approach was that I was limited to the English language spoken with an Irish-French accent, whereas Pauline was ministering and interpreting in the languages of these different countries. I was trying to adapt to a new culture for a couple of weeks. Pauline had already absorbed and lived in that culture with national recognition.

I could write about the cold dark winter days of my first visit to Finland, travelling in a fairly old Volkswagen "Beetle" along icy snow-covered tree-lined roads, with Pauline and her short-term co-worker to some church or meeting. I remember my surprise when I learned that part of her Bible-school teaching programme included New Testament Greek. I kept clear of any use of it in my preaching!

We often spoke French together and enjoyed a few Irish stories where she even attempted to imitate my native Irish brogue.

During the 70's and 80's in Britain and much of Western Europe, there was evidence of an economic boom based on E.U.predictions Scandinavia seemed to offer lucrative market potential. At that time male dominance of executive appointments was being challenged. Some international companies, with their eyes on Northern Europe, were looking for effective representation, male or female, with ABILITY, academic and linguistic, AVAILABILITY, free to travel without family restrictions, and ACCEPTABILITY in terms of culture and adaptation. I have no doubt that Pauline would have met all these requirements and could have embraced a very different lifestyle than that which emerges from missionary life in the adopted countries which figure in this book.

The text which comes to mind is "The gifts and calling of the Lord are without repentance (regrets). Rom 11 v 29.

Pauline has chosen well. She has laid up "treasures in heaven". May all who read this inspiring account of her ministries do likewise.

**J. Cecil Young**
*Former British and French Director of E.C.M.*
*and accredited Baptist Minister.*

# INTRODUCTION

Some years ago I came across a packet of washing powder in the home of some friends in Finland. It was called "Mini-risk" and was gentle on the skin and on the environment – hence the name. However, the name hit me, not on my skin but in my soul! Is this the name of our Christianity? Are we happy to warm a pew and praise the Lord on Sundays and say, "Lord I will do anything for you so long as I don't have to get out of my comfort zone"? The very fact that I was in Finland at the time, often living out of a suitcase, visiting whatever churches would have me, to stir up interest in mission in general and mission in Europe in particular, indicated that I had got out of the comfort zone myself. In fact, apart from leaving home and country to follow Jesus, I had already been on a few adventures in Communist Europe on the Lord's business. So I couldn't really fit myself into the mini-risk zone. I started preaching on the subject of "Mini-risk Christianity" and challenged Christians to take instead the "Maxi-risk" line that Jesus Himself had taken. I have been living a comparatively maxi-risk life for many years now, and despite the cost I can only recommend it, as it brings with it maxi-blessing! The title of this book has been changed to be more relevant to those not familiar with the Mini-risk products, but when originally published in Swedish (in a slightly shorter version) it was called "Maxi-risk: My Adventures with Jesus in Many Languages" The subtitle underlines the probable uniqueness of my ministry, in that I have preached, taught or given public testimony in a dozen languages and managed some conversation or stumbling testimony in a few more. This also explains the many references in the book to a "maxi-risk" lifestyle.

I was recently amused to be challenged in a book to "re-invent" amongst other things, my lifestyle. I can testify to the fact that without any effort from me, beyond obedience, the Lord has been "re-inventing" my lifestyle over and over for the past 45 years. I have lived in six countries, visited many others, and had to change language, culture, climate, food and circumstances many times over. It has been both scary and fun! I am not naturally an adventurous person, but knowing I am in Jesus' hand, led by His Spirit, makes me brave way beyond my natural inclinations.

I am aware that the pernicious little word "I" comes in rather often in this book, but then it is a personal story. Our lives have to be lived in a personal relationship with God and with others. Please look at God's work, His grace and mercy, beyond all the personal story, because it is He who shall have all the glory. I do not claim to be a writer of merit, I just write as I speak.

As the chapters that follow may sometimes leave the reader confused as to timing I will give a list of dates and places where I lived, to refer back to:

1960-62    Varkaus, Finland – teaching English
1962-64    Bible Training Institute, Glasgow
1964-65    Church of Finland Inland Mission college, Pieksämäki, Finland

1965-69  Helsinki Bible School, Helsinki, Finland
1969-75  Espoo, (near Helsinki) Finland – travelling
in Finland and beyond.
1975-81  Mariestad, Sweden – travelling all over the
Nordic countries.
1981-84  Kandern, Black Forest, Germany – ECM's
European office.
1984-87  Aurich, Northwest Germany – church work.
1987-90  China – teaching English
1990-91  Hong Kong – administrative work.
1991-93  York – work with Chinese students.
1993-98  Hungary – work amongst Chinese market
people.
1998-99  Sabbatical year in Finland
1999-03  Manchester – work amongst Chinese
academics.
Aug 2003 Retirement.

Visits to Eastern Europe were made between 1966 and 1984.

From 1969 to 1987 I worked with the European Christian Mission, supported financially from 1976 onwards by Fria Missionsförbundet (The Swedish-speaking Free Evangelical Church in Finland). From 1987 I was supported entirely by the church in Finland, though I also had prayer partners in several other countries, especially in the UK.

## SECTION ONE
### Who am I?

---

# 1

---

## EARLY YEARS

### Home life

I was called Paul until I was born, as my parents wanted a brother for their first daughter, but they never held it against me that I turned out to be a girl! My mother used to tell me how, whilst still in the local Hospital, the nurses one day, whilst she went for a bath, bathed me too, arranged my little auburn curls, and put me in her bed with a folded letter propped up in front, as if I was reading a book. Was that prophetic? I became a "bookworm." In fact we were eventually three girls and treated with love and equality - absolutely no favourites, and a no-nonsense upbringing. Discipline was more by words than by smacks, and a threat of reduction in our modest spending money was an effective method of getting us to obey! When we were old enough to take responsibility we helped with housework - a small cleaning job before school each day, taking turns to set or clear the table, wash or dry the dishes, learning to cook and bake etc. I am so grateful for all this, as many girls miss out on it these days. Not that my parents were perfect, but although we were not a "touchy-feely" family I was aware of my parents' love for each other (they could disagree but I never heard them use angry words at each other) and for us (sometimes appreciated only in later years). I considered myself the "black sheep" because I could be moody, rude and grousy, - yes, I certainly had a temper, but what else can you expect with auburn hair?! On the other hand, my mother called me the clown of the family - always ready with a pun, a joke, a funny voice or a bit of clowning. In fact, as a family we had plenty of humour. The tension was broken in many a situation by a quip from one or other of us, which changed frowns into laughter.

There are biblical examples of favouritism within a family, e.g. Isaac and Rachel each had their favourite son. Then Jacob loved Joseph as his favourite, which caused bitterness and suffering later on. I have seen families today where a child feels both glad and guilty that he/she is a parent's or grandparent's favourite, and other children who feel rejected and angry because they are not the favourite. Comparison is equally bad, such as in: "Why can't you be like your sister?" In our family there was no such favouritism or comparison, (just natural sibling rivalry) and for this I am so grateful. Each child needs to be accepted and valued for him- or herself.

Dad was gentle, though firm, even stubborn. He had left school at 14 after the death of his father and then of his brother in the First World War, as he had to support his mother and four sisters. He studied at evening classes to complete his education and was very good with figures, using them in his job, and teaching us to do sums in our heads as a game at Sunday lunch. But he was also an inventor who created useful things for the home, but also many games, which brought endless fun to children's and family parties. I think my inventive streak came from him. One of his rather quaint sayings, which showed his own values of marital faithfulness, and in this way impressed it on us, was: "Never monkey with another monkey's monkey." Biblically that translates into "Do not commit adultery."

In contrast, Mum had gone to college and qualified as a teacher. She had also been active as a Girl Guide leader for many years, and had received the Silver Fish (highest Guide award of those days, like today's Queen's Guide) from the hand of Lady Baden Powell herself. Mum was on the one hand a diplomat, on the other a strong-willed lady. My sisters tell me she dominated them in various ways. I never noticed this trait in her - maybe because my will was just as strong! For example, I started learning the piano from a family friend at four years old, and was pretty good by the age of eight. But then we had dry rot under the lounge floor and I couldn't practise for a few weeks. When the piano was reachable again I had decided not to continue. Sheer madness, as I saw years later, but I had made up my mind and not even Mum could move me.

My father had two weeks holiday a year – usual at that time – one week to be taken in April, the other in August. The April week my parents took on their own, farming us out to relatives and school friends until we were old enough to cope on our own at home. It was a good arrangement and we all enjoyed the different kind of week. In August we would go to the seaside together, usually to Hoylake on the Wirral or Prestatyn in North Wales. A day out every year in May saw us picnicking in Monsal Dale in Derbyshire and gathering lilies-of-the-valley, which grew there in abundance.

My wartime memories are very few: being carried down to the air-raid shelter; sitting looking at the tousled black hair of a new baby sister; visiting Grandma's partly bombed out house - fortunately she had been away when the bomb fell. During and after the War (WW2) things were scarce. We had ration books for tea, butter, margarine, sugar, bread, sweets and clothes. Our next-door neighbours drank strong tea without sugar, whereas we drank weak tea with sugar. This was very convenient, as we could exchange tea and sugar, and both families had enough of the drink they enjoyed. We would take our pocket money to the sweet shop on Saturdays to get our two ounces of sweets - usually boiled sweets or dolly mixtures. I didn't want to eat them all at once, but if they were there..... so I hid them in some corner or other to spread the enjoyment. The trouble was that I found real hideaways and then forgot where they were. A sticky bag of sweets would turn up behind the piano or settee weeks later! They called me "squirrel"!

The above-mentioned Grandma, Mum's mother was the only grandparent I knew, as the others had died before I was born. She died when I was ten, so my memories of her are rather vague by now. She had had a hard life and was a Victorian granny, not the cuddly sort one might have wished for. In fact, our family generally speaking, though caring, was not "cuddly" and I had to learn as an adult how important touch is in showing comfort and care.

When we were quite small we got a kitten and had to learn to look after him. Next door had a kitten of similar age and they used to play together, until they grew up and became less friendly. They had a remarkable truce if either family was away. If we found their cat on our doormat we knew they were out, and if ours walked into their kitchen and ate from the same plate as their cat, they knew we were out. Otherwise the one-time playmates were sworn enemies.

We had a big old wireless (as radios were then called) and we listened to the news from the warfront each day, though I didn't understand much of what it was about. I had just grown up with the fact that there was a war on. So when the fighting ended I supposed the news bulletins would end too - after all, they only talked about war, and I remember being quite surprised that The News continued. When the War ended (VE Day) there was a big celebration outside the Town Hall in Sale, though the building itself was merely a shell, having been hit by a bomb. It was the first time we were out late as the whole family joined the crowd. I was six at the time.

Christmas is a fun time for children, and so it was for us. We would take our stockings into our parents' bedroom to open and find the welcome little luxuries such as a tangerine, some chocolate, an apron etc. Once the youngest had cracked the Father Christmas story we started to fill stockings for Mum and Dad too, so the fun could continue for years. As students we then hurried out to do our post delivery round - students were taken on in those days, and there was a delivery on Christmas Day - before going to church. When my elder sister got her first job and we others put our pocket money in, we managed to buy a "Teasmade" bedside light, clock and tea-maker. This was hidden next door until the right moment, and was a total surprise to delighted parents. I might add that it was really a present to ourselves, as we always had to take it in turns to take Mum and Dad a cuppa on Saturday and Sunday mornings - not a welcome chore for young people who hate getting up early. Weekend mornings became more pleasant when the tea made itself!

## School life

If I could be sometimes awkward at home, outside I was a paragon of good behaviour and young maturity, always being supposed to be older than I really was, and seen as very responsible. It turned out I had been endowed with high intelligence, which showed itself early. Learning from my older sister, who had already started school, I could read well by the time I started school just turned five. So I sat in a corner reading books from Class Five whilst my contemporaries learned their ABC. It meant I was bored and my parents decided our youngest sister should not learn before she started school. Just before she turned five she duly trotted off for her first day at School. Coming home that first day she declared she wasn't going again. When asked the reason she replied, "We didn't learn to read or write!" It runs in the family! So from the start I was up at the top of the class with two other girls. In Class Three at primary school

I remember getting a prize for finding 57 words out of "Christmas Tree", way above the next highest score. I have been a person of words ever since. Words of one sort or another, one dialect or another, one language or another, have been my delight. Fortunately I never learned bad words or bad language! And the integrity I learned, first from my parents, then from the Bible, was far more important than any amount of intelligence. (Some master-criminals have been highly intelligent too!) Later, as a Christian, I have loved to use both words and life to teach the Word of God.

Having passed the 11-plus exam I moved up to Sale Grammar School for Girls, just a few minutes walk from home. There too, I excelled until the teenage blues meant I lost some enthusiasm higher up the school, and actually failed an exam. I don't know when I decided I wanted to become a teacher, but as soon as I started French I wanted to be a language teacher. In the second year we did Latin (I was in the academic class by then, of course), which I also enjoyed. The following year the choice was between continuing Latin and starting German. Of course I was to take Latin, as I was university material - or that is what parents and teachers said. I, however, decided Latin was a dead language and German was more interesting as you could speak it, so I would take German! Thinking back I am amazed that a 12-yr old could hold her own against the 'powers that be' and actually win the language battle. Did I mention my strong will??? I took German, and never looked back. (I caught up on the compulsory Latin in the sixth form.) If I now look back I see God's hand in all this, but at that time I didn't know Him and wasn't asking Him. He knew me, however, and was leading and preparing me for His future service.

Another example of my pioneer spirit that showed itself early, I remember, concerned the film "Mandy", about a deaf girl. The film had partly been made at the School for the Deaf, where my aunt and uncle headed up the primary department. We had been to watch the film being made and my innate "teaching gene" was fascinated by the methods of teaching deaf children to speak. We went as a family to watch the film when it came out. Months later it came round again to our local cinema and I wanted to go and see it again. The rest of the family thought once was enough, but I was so fascinated by the teaching that I insisted it was terribly important to me, and eventually was allowed to go on my own. I think I even considered become a teacher of the deaf for some time after that.

Going to the cinema alone was one thing, travelling by train to visit relatives in Scotland was another, and at 12 years of age I was mortified to have a luggage label tied to my cardigan giving my name and address. Of course I tucked it inside so nobody could see I was a "parcel". All went well and my parents began to have confidence in my travelling, so just before my 17th birthday I was allowed to visit my penfriend in Germany. I was not alone, but my travelling companion was a 14-yr old German girl who had been brought over by a friend and needed a "responsible companion" to travel back with. At 16 I was considered to fit that bill. We sat on the overnight train through Holland and Germany. It was so crowded we couldn't sleep until all the others got out in Hannover and we lay down, waking only when the ticket inspector came. It turned out we had slept through our station, Braunschweig, (Brunswick) and were on our way to the next stop, which was on the East German border. Oh dear! It was nearly an unexpectedly early trip into communist zones. All ended happily as we caught the next train back.

I went to school with my penfriend. In post-war Germany the schools left standing were used to double capacity, so we went one week at 6am and the other week at 2pm. I certainly learnt a lot of German language and culture, made some amusing mistakes, and was taken sightseeing by a neighbour who had lost a leg in the war. The English teacher asked me to read from their English book – this was to be the genuine article, a native English speaker. But with my slight northern accent I pronounced "path" and "lamp" with the same open "a", which was not the same as the Queen's English that was taught in Germany, and the teacher informed me that I was wrong!! I explained that I was right in my part of the world, but I had lost her confidence. My penfriend and I travelled back to England with her whole class. She in turn amused us by saying she put "customs" on her apple pie. When corrected to "custard" she insisted that no, that is what you go through when you come into the country!

A few years later, on another student travel adventure going from Germany to a pen-friend in the south of France I ended up in Paris instead. I had not been aware that the train split into two at some point and I was on the wrong half. It was night-time and no ticket inspector came before the split to find that I was sitting in a wrong carriage. However, when the inspector did come, he was very helpful and advised me how to cross Paris, send a telegram, and get the next train down south. These little adventures in my teens prepared me for much bigger ones in later life.

After a summer job in Germany I returned to England hitch-hiking with an American girl. One moment we were on the back of an applecart, the next in a comfortable limousine, the next in a racy sports car. Arriving in Brussels quite late in the evening the Youth Hostel had been booked out for months, as the big "Exposition" was on in Brussels. But we arrived just before the doors closed at 10pm and were given places that had not been taken. Next morning we looked round some of the Exhibition before moving on to London. From the overnight boat we got to London in the morning and went straight to book standing tickets for My Fair Lady, which was playing with its original cast, Julie Andrews, Rex Harrison, Stanley Holloway. Seats had, of course, been booked out months ahead, but standing tickets could only be bought on the day. I already knew the songs as a friend had got the record from America, so I was thrilled to see the action that went along with them.

**Music and Literature**

Music has been a joy to me through my life in one form or another. As mentioned earlier, I learned to play the piano at an early age, but gave it up because I didn't like practising. I did pick it up again a little at Bible college, where I learned to play hymns and fill in chords with the left hand. This was useful when travelling in different churches, where there was sometimes nobody to play the piano or harmonium in the little chapel, so I could step in and accompany the hymns. Today I can pick out a tune best by ear and fill in some harmony.

Having left the piano behind in primary school age I had the chance to learn the violin at grammar school. Unfortunately I had been given a very poor violin, which even the teacher couldn't make sing. But I pressed on, had some fun, and we even joined with other schools in an orchestra. However, when I left school the violin also was left behind. I have also played a little on the recorder and guitar. This last was useful for meetings, when I would introduce myself with a song, which I could accompany myself, though my range of chords is strictly limited.

The one "instrument" I carried with me was my voice. I have sung duets with one or other of my sisters, and once I left home, sung mostly on my own, though also with church choirs or similar groups. I love singing, whether at home for my own pleasure and to praise Jesus, or as a ministry in church. I was once thanked for my preaching the previous Sunday - but I hadn't preached. The person then remembered I had sung, but the words of the song had meant so much to her that for her I had preached. I loved that, because when I sing for others I want it to be a message rather than a performance. The acoustics are important too, of course, and I like to go into an empty church sometimes and sing my heart out to the Lord, at the same time enjoying the sound of my powerful voice in good surroundings, without anyone being able to say I am 'showing off'!

Of course I have enjoyed other people's music too. As I did 'O' level (now GCSE) music I was on the rota at school to get a free ticket to Hallé concerts at the Free Trade Hall in Manchester. But often on a Wednesday I would waylay the music teacher after school, and if no-one else had claimed the ticket I could have it. I would rush home for a bite of tea, then catch the train into Manchester and thoroughly enjoy whatever the programme was. It didn't bother me at all that I went alone - the streets were safer in those days - and as the ticket was free it only cost me the train fare and programme price, a shilling all told. If I went to other concerts, or the ballet, which I also loved, I would stand at the back of "the gods" at the cheapest ticket price. All this stopped when I left home and concerts were not so easy to find, or were very expensive and beyond my pocket.

Literature appreciation, on the other hand, is something I have never been enthusiastic about. Oh I read books by the dozen, becoming a frequent visitor at the local library, but poetry, Shakespeare, classical novels - I had gut feelings about them but couldn't analyse and appraise them as I should, and thus failed my A-level English. This meant the bottom dropped out of my world, as I didn't get into the university of my first choice. For some time I was completely lost, almost drowning, claiming I never wanted to go to university anyway and looking round for an alternative. Then my second choice university, Nottingham, accepted me to do German and French, and life looked up again. And it was at Nottingham that I found a personal faith in Jesus. (More about that later.) This faith and the Christian Union, building on the values learnt at home, helped me avoid the normal pitfalls and sins of student life. I felt that I now had solid ground under my feet, a direction to move in and a Friend to take me through.

But literature was still a struggle - why can't you just study language when you study languages?? German literature was hard, but I could just about cope with it. French literature was sexy and with my rather "Victorian" upbringing, and also as a new Christian I couldn't appreciate it. So again failure was on the table and I had to drag French Literature through my third year, failing then too. For struggling students God will often help through success in exams. Perhaps I needed to fail to show me that I couldn't rely on my own brains to get me through life, I needed to see my weaknesses and I needed God. (Not that I recall being proud of my intelligence, it was something I just took for granted, couldn't always understand why other people didn't grasp things as quickly as I did.) The difference between the A-level failure, when I wasn't a Christian, and the degree failure was striking. On the first occasion I had felt the bottom had dropped out of my world and I was drifting in an unknown sea. The second time, after a good weep, even my Christian friends were surprised that I could so quickly say "I did my best, and God must have a purpose in this." As indeed He had.

I had applied to spend a year abroad teaching English before settling into my chosen profession as teacher in Britain. The only country open for this at the time was Finland. I know now that most other countries do it too, but God wanted me in Finland, so He shut all other doors. As it was only to be for a year I decided that even the unknown realm of Finland could be endured, as the job of teaching adults really appealed to me. Nottingham university offered me the opportunity (not given to all failed students) to study on my own at home and retake the French Literature exams the following year. It seemed stupid not to accept this, so I put Finland on hold, spent a month on a course in France to revive my flagging interest in that language, returned home and got a job for a few months. Study wasn't easy on this hated subject, but eventually I got through and was awarded my B.A. And during that year the Lord turned my life around to new horizons - mission.

Unbeknown to me, my non-academic intelligence was about to launch into a programme of practical language learning through which I could spread the Gospel, teach the Word of God and encourage Christians to share their faith through mission. This was to happen in many countries and many languages and in my opinion has been a far better use of my intelligence than, for example doing research into some dusty subject. Several people have suggested I should have been an interpreter with the UN, but that is saying only what others said and not using my own words! I never set out to learn a dozen or so languages, they just came one by one as the Lord led me in His work and a new language was needed to communicate with people and share the Word of God. Because of my God-given talent I had the capacity to learn these languages, but many people suppose it was "easy" for me. I can say that every language has its story of how I learnt it, but every one needed effort and persistence and I have shed tears of frustration over almost every language at some point, when it seemed impossible to make progress.

# 2

## GOD IN MY LIFE

Psalm 139 tells of God knowing us even before we were born. It is a comfort to realise this and to see how He leads even before we know Him. My parents were good-living people. They rarely attended church but "did their best" for God. We certainly learned good moral values from their example and we were taught to say bedtime prayers. My first experience of God's presence was actually when I was kneeling by my bed saying my prayers one summer evening. The little top window was open, and I suddenly felt that God had come in through that window and was there with me. On Sunday afternoons our parents wanted some peace for a nap, so we children were sent to a local Sunday school which, although not evangelical, taught us about the Bible. And we lapped it up. In fact, when the Manchester Sunday School Union held annual Bible exams we were there in the extra classes, and then getting top marks. Some years there was also a Music and Arts Festival and there too, we were at the forefront. The little certificates we gained for singing, recitation, writing and doll making were reward enough for all the hard work we put in.

All this Christian influence was fun and interesting, but not something that really lived inside me. Of course I considered myself a Christian, knowing so much about Jesus and the Bible, and respecting it. But when I got to university that idea changed. David Sheppard (later bishop of Liverpool) was at that time (1957) known as captain of the England cricket team, but had just been ordained and was invited by the Christian Union to take a meeting in Nottingham. Two of my dig-mates and I were rather taken with the idea of seeing a famous sports star, so decided to go and hear him. I don't remember what he said, but through him God spoke to my heart and I realised Jesus had died for me personally so I wanted to thank Him and ask Him into my life. By the end of the meeting it was not David Sheppard who was the star in my life, but Jesus. I remember saying to the girl who counselled me, "I was a Christian before, but this is different." Indeed it was. This brought me into contact with the Christian Union, and friends there helped me grow into the Christian life and a personal relationship with Jesus. Only a couple of months into this new life I went to Germany for a compulsory term's study at Freiburg University, together with the only other girl in my year, Pat. She was already a Christian and through her encouragement we got involved in the local Christian Union, which provided both spiritual help and social relaxation. In fact, German was the first language in which I prayed aloud at a prayer meeting!

My ambition to become a teacher of German and French in Britain had not changed, but now I was going to use it for Jesus. I had my plans! During the years at university I went to Christian Easter conferences for students at The Hayes in Swanwick. They were good times and the year I was at home afterwards I realised I would miss it, not knowing a live church at home. So I looked around and found there was an Easter

Conference at Heightside, the HQ of the European Christian Mission (ECM) in Rawtenstall, just the other side of Manchester. I booked and turned up in pouring rain. On the last bus I slipped my shoes and stockings off and waded barefoot up the long drive turned into a river, towards the impressive old house on the hill that was for many years the centre of the Mission. The lady who opened the door did look rather surprised. As yet I knew nothing about ECM or about the Lord's plans for me. The main conference speaker was Rev. Ian Coffey and the theme: JESUS IS LORD. We sang a little chorus several times during the weekend:

Lay your life on the altar for God,
He is calling for you today
Lay your life on the altar for God
This moment the Master obey.
The fields of the harvest are white
But the labourers are scattered and few.
Lay your life on the altar for God,
He is calling for you, for you.

I sang along happily with the others until Saturday evening, when it hit me full force: He is calling for you, Pauline, for you! At the invitation to stand some force pulled me to my feet as tears streamed down my face. When the meeting finished and people started saying encouraging things to me I just pushed my way out, ran up to my room and cried the rest out on my knees. Pauline was cried out, all her ambitions of being a teacher laid on the altar for God, - my Isaac, I later called it, being the thing I held most dear in life - and Jesus was cried in, with His plans for Pauline to be a missionary. "I can't, Lord" I explained. "I could stand up and teach German, but I can't stand up and speak about Jesus. But Lord, if You want me to, here I am, use me." It is interesting to note with hindsight, that, like Isaac, my "teaching gene" was blessed and given back to me to use for the

Lord. And some years later I caught myself saying to someone, "I don't care so much about teaching languages, teaching about Jesus is what I love most." God had taken me at my word and turned around my attitudes.

There on my knees in my room at the conference I didn't hear any words that I recall, but after spending some time with the Lord I had put the three important issues of life into His hands -

a - the question of my career

b - my money, much or little

c - the question of marriage, whether or not and if so, to whom.

Looking back, I realise that if these areas are not under His control then we are not all His. In fact, if I made the decisions in these areas God would then have very little of me left to control. I was so glad that at this early stage of my life I could put them into His hands, where they are in safe-keeping. I will comment on the outworking of these issues in a moment. When sometimes asked if I have "received the Second Blessing" (a rather old term now,) or been "baptised in the Spirit" I think back to that moment of my life. I believe that if the Holy Spirit fills us it is to bring us to this full commitment - an uplifting experience of joy is an optional extra. For me this lasting commitment was accompanied by tears rather than a sense of euphoria, which can soon wear off. My commitment has never "worn off", though I have sometimes struggled to keep my offering on the altar.

Coming back to the other people at the conference I could explain to the ECM folk that four things were now clear to me.

1. All my life is for Jesus

2. He wants me to be a missionary

3. It will be in Europe

4. It will be through ECM

They were worried about this last one, thinking I said it out of duty and they pointed out that only the first one was important for now. Yes, I said, but I know God has said all these things. And He had, although I needed faith to see all fulfilled, as it was nine years before I actually moved full-time into ECM. God is careful about His preparation. My first thought was Bible college, but when I applied to the Bible Training Institute in Glasgow (one of the few that at that time recognised Europe as a mission field) it was full for the coming year, so I decided to go ahead with the plans already made for a year in Finland in the meantime, not knowing that this too was in God's long-term plan.

To return to the three areas of life that I committed to the Lord. They have worked out as follows:

**Career:** I gave up my ambition to become a teacher, but have ended up teaching in one way or another most of my life. Sometimes teaching English as a Foreign Language was the best way of reaching people, and other times I have explained the Bible to individuals, groups or churches full of people. My missionary service, chosen by God, has used the natural gifts He laid in me - the joy of helping people to understand things they didn't know before. Yes, I gave up the safe German-teaching career I had been planning, but the Bible teaching I have done, amongst other things, has been more interesting than anything I could have planned for myself.

**Money:** as a language teacher in Britain I would have earned far more than the minimal support I received "living by faith" as a missionary. (This was before the days of regulated missionary salaries.) Fortunately I didn't come from a rich family and had been brought up to be careful and frugal. So I just put this into practice for the rest of my life. But God's mathematics are quite beyond me. Most of the time I have tithed, sometimes given large offerings on top of that, as the Lord has prompted me, and yet He has somehow paid me back so I don't understand why I still have a bank balance in the black. I have always lived within my income, never gone into debt or bought anything I couldn't afford. I was once asked by a non-Christian relative how I was doing financially and said I was doing fine "But I thought you only got 'peanuts'" the scornful tone continued. "Yes," I smiled, "but peanuts with Jesus is enough." And so it has been.

**Marriage:** many people seem to assume that I decided not to marry when I became a missionary. This is not true. As mentioned above I put the matter into God's hands, it was to be His decision, not mine. I walked day by day with Him, sometimes wondering whether a life partner would be around the corner, sometimes praying for one, but always putting it back into His hands, since following Jesus was my first priority. It hasn't always been easy. Even if I was mostly relaxed about the matter, friends, particularly Christian friends, were keen to find somebody for me. "Haven't you found a husband yet?" was a frequent question which became irritating with time. I am often saddened by the attitude of married church people to unmarried people over 30, making them second-class citizens. One preacher even said: "You must find a husband, so that you will become a 'person'." (- a little difficult to translate as this was not said in English.) Thinking about it later I supposed he was thinking of Adam and Eve being one flesh, God's creation of humanity, but he had forgotten the "the two become one" not two halves. And there is all the New Testament teaching about singleness, and indeed the great examples of Jesus and Paul. Were they not truly people? Yes, Christians can be much more hurtful than worldly people sometimes.

Looking back now, I see that I could not have done the ministry I have done if I had been married and had a family. Moving from country to country, integrating into the local cultures, submerging myself in the languages - all this would have been impossible with a home language and culture to return to each night. I know families go to the mission field, but usually only to one country and culture. And so many come home for the children's schooling. I was available for God's work in the way Paul said, thinking about what the Lord wanted instead of what a family might want and need. I have met some arguing families and been grateful for being single. I have met harmonious couples and been just a bit envious. Mostly I have just got on with the Lord's work. Keeping the right priorities is so important - following Jesus first, all other matters second.

I have become very international, and I sometimes manage to do the wrong thing in the wrong country! Yet God has helped me to adapt and be accepted as "one of us" in several countries and cultures, particularly in Europe. In China, of course, I stood out like the proverbial sore thumb, especially as I am tall and fair, and lived in the south, where the people are small and dark. Early on, in Finland, a friend was not very polite about foreigners on one occasion. "Thank you!" I said, at which she turned to me in surprise and said "Oh, I don't think of you as a foreigner." When I told Swedish-speaking friends in Finland that I had described myself in Norway as "an English Finn from Sweden" - I was living in Sweden at the time - I was corrected. "You are not just a Finn (which to them means Finnish-speaking), you are one of us too!" And in Germany, when my sister was coming to visit, someone said how nice, we would have an international meeting. I asked if it wasn't international with me there. Again the look of surprise. "Oh no, you are one of us!" It got complicated in Hungary as I had to explain to those who asked where I was from or what I was doing. "Well, listen carefully," I would answer, "I am English, supported by a Swedish-speaking church in Finland, working amongst the Chinese in Hungary." Rather international?

There have been many lessons to learn on the way. Missionaries, in fact all Christians, are not flawless. I have let the Lord down many times, but He has never let me down. The only time I remember having real doubts about God was in Finland one summer. I felt lonely and couldn't feel God's presence even in my prayers. (Most Christians seem to experience this at some time.) I went for a walk out in the country. A big cloud covered the sun as I walked along crying, "Where are You, Lord?" As I looked up at the cloud a ray of sunshine peeped through a tiny hole in the centre of the cloud. It quickly disappeared, but that was God's reassuring smile to me, as if He was graciously saying, "I am still here, and when the cloud passes you will feel my warmth and light again." The cloud passed and the sun shone again, and my cloud of doubt passed too. Since then I have always been sure of God's presence even when it was as from behind a dark cloud.

With a strong will and a pioneer spirit, and lots of ideas and initiative, it has sometimes been difficult to live with myself, and occasionally difficult to interact with others, though usually I get on well with people. I have had times when I have neglected taking time with the Lord, which has led to times of depression, criticism of others and feeling sorry for myself. The Lord has restored me with the sense of His arms around me and His goodness drawing me back. I have had times of great loneliness, working on my own, (though meeting many people), travelling on my own, and yet I have friends in many countries who are always glad to see me. I have sometimes even disliked my strong personality, but have learned to accept and appreciate (the Bible calls it love) the person God created me to be, warts and all, which helps me also to accept and love other people!

SECTION TWO
Finland

---
3
---

NEW EXPERIENCES

Hardly ever heard of it, far away in the north - is it behind the Iron Curtain? Although often referred to as part of Scandinavia Finland technically does not belong to those countries and is only included in "Fenno-Scandinavia", "the Nordic countries" or more vaguely "Northern Europe". Linguistically and ethnically it is quite different, although politically it was a part of Sweden for hundreds of years, before becoming an autonomous province of Russia for a century. It was only in 1917 that it first became independent. I travelled to Finland via Sweden with a number of other British Council teachers. Sweden still had left-hand traffic like Britain, though the steering wheel was on the left, which made it easy for them to change over to right-hand traffic some time later. On arrival in Helsinki we were treated to a meal in a good hotel. I had got hold of an old-fashioned phrase-book before I left, which gave some vocabulary in Finnish. It looked so impossible that I quickly put it down, but did store one phrase in my mind for emergencies. After the hotel meal was the moment to use it. Beckoning a waitress I asked her "Missä on käymälä?" To my delight she showed me to the toilet. But when I got back a girl who knew some Finnish told me the word was more appropriate for a lavatory on a train or in an outhouse, not a fine hotel! So what? It worked!! We had a few days of orientation before going our separate ways. I was allotted to a smallish town called Varkaus a bit east of central Finland. Centred round the wood, cellulose and paper-making industry its main firm was Ahlström, a Swedish-speaking founder, and therefore it had an elite of Swedish-speaking executives in the midst of a very Finnish-speaking area. (About 6% of Finns have Swedish as their mother-tongue.) I travelled up by night train arriving very early in the morning. My carriage should have been put in a siding, where I could sleep until 8.am, but in Helsinki I found this would not happen and I had to get out when we arrived at 4.30 and sit on the station waiting to be met. Sitting there in the late summer morning I watched the sun rise, and saw engines shunting goods wagons to and fro. The engines were wood-fired and had a bulbous chimney designed to catch the sparks - fascinating insights into my new surroundings right from the beginning. The secretary of the Finnish-British Society I was to teach for met me at the arranged time, and was horrified to find I had been waiting so long. He showed me my flat, with a large living-room to hold my classes, then took me to the local shops. He stopped to talk to a friend and I listened to them. The words sounded like the bit of Swedish I had once learnt, but the intonation was quite different, yet the few Finnish words I had heard didn't sound like this either. I discovered this was Finland-Swedish, the language of the 6% minority, basically the Swedish language with flat Finnish intonation and some of its own words and phrases.

I had been able to obtain the names of two middle-aged Christian ladies in the town, who had written to tell me a little about it and welcome me. They were both engineers in

Ahlström, the big company that practically ran Varkaus. Being Finnish-speaking women in those positions usually held by Swedish-speaking men made them very unusual. Leena and Anna-Maija had been friends from university days and now shared a house just behind the big Lutheran church. It became a second home to me, and they also introduced me to the youth group at church. I was asked to speak to the young people, whose English was nowhere near as good as it often is today. So I wrote in English, had Leena translate it, and spent a few days practising the pronunciation. Although it is one of the most difficult languages to learn from the vocabulary and grammar point of view, Finnish is an easy language to read, as it is pronounced almost without exception as it is written - so long as you know the correct pronunciation of each letter. So there was I, a month in the country and giving a talk in Finnish. Even though my pronunciation of t,k,p was still rather English everyone understood what I was saying - everyone except me, of course! Four months later, giving another talk at a New Year youth camp, I helped with the translation and understood what I was saying! I had made progress.

There were lots of new things to get used to. I ate twice a day at the canteen for Ahlström white collar workers - that was part of my salary - so had to get used to different mealtimes (11.30am for lunch and 5.00pm for dinner) and different food. With no supermarkets I had to learn to ask for what I wanted in the shops - a useful way of learning the language, helped by friendly assistants. The teaching was also new to me, as I had no training or qualifications other than having English as my mother tongue and an innate desire to teach (my mother and aunt had been teachers so it was "in the genes"). It was a bit hard-going at first, as the Finns were mostly very reticent and afraid to speak for fear of being wrong. I felt they were saying "Teacher will now teach us to speak fluent English, and in the process we don't need to open our mouths!" The older people were more fun and more forthcoming. At their first lesson a group of executives who called themselves "The Lazy Boys" arrived, all but one. He came a few minutes late, with a carnation for the teacher. (Flowers are given individually in a country where they are very expensive.) This prompted the comment from one of the others: "Six men, one gentleman." Although the Finns in those days addressed each other with titles - teacher, director, bank manager etc. - we went for equality in the English classes, using only Mr. Mrs. and Miss. So I didn't know who was what in society. One day in a fairly elementary class I smilingly but chidingly corrected a "Mr." who made a common mistake when he should have known better. He laughed with me, but the others disappeared behind their books with embarrassment. Afterwards someone asked me "Do you know who he is?" I didn't. "He is the assistant mayor!!" I was told with awe - a very elevated position in the small town. I stuck to my guns - he is a "Mr." to me, and a student who made a mistake in his English. He and I remained friends.

Actually, as the English teacher in town I also had an elevated position. There were three important posts - Mayor, Vicar and English teacher! Everybody seemed to know who I was, which was both encouraging and unnerving. As previous teachers had either learned Swedish (and circulated amongst the elite) or nothing, my efforts to learn Finnish were much appreciated by everybody. Added to that, I was the first female teacher in the Finnish-British Society in Varkaus, so my place in history was assured!!

Another new thing was the sauna. In those days you could only find a sauna in England at the Finnish Seamen's Mission in London, and I hadn't been down there to try it. Another Christian lady, Ester, came with me to show me the ropes. Undress, take a shower, and enter the oven - well it felt like an oven. My first reaction was to think, "If hell is hotter than this I'm glad I'm saved!!!" Because it was in a block of flats, electrically heated and with only a shower for cooling down it was only a poor foretaste of the saunas I later encountered -

wood-heated cabins by the lakeside, where you could beat yourself with fresh leafy birch twigs to encourage sweating, drop into the lake to cool down after the sweating, and then scrub each other's backs. In winter you could even roll in the snow, which I did, and some brave souls would take a dip through a hole in the ice, which I didn't.

The first six months went well, I was rapidly falling in love with everything Finnish, and then came the time I had to decide whether to stay another year. Bible College was lined up and I had informed the British Council that I would not be staying, when a chance remark made me rethink. Should I? I wrote to the British Council asking if I could change my mind, and asked the Lord to guide me through their answer. The answer came - one day later would really have been too late. "So now you have to decide," said one of my friends. I was thrown into a flurry of uncertainty - I had to decide? I thought this was God's answer. For several days I was in a bad mood because I was tossed to and fro by doubts and responsibility. One evening, as I walked home, it was as if the Lord was walking beside me and I argued with Him.

"I don't know what to do."

"You asked for an answer and I gave it."

"Yes, but Lord, I'm not sure...."

"You asked and I answered."

"Yes but...."

"I gave you the answer."

The patient but insistent voice in my mind's ear eventually convinced me. By the time I reached home I had accepted the Lord's answer and relaxed. How stupid we sometimes are to doubt when He clearly shows us what to do. So I stayed for a second year in the country I had already fallen in love with, making more friends, learning more of the language and culture and background, not realising to what extent this was all part of God's plan for the future. Little did I know I would later live in Scandinavia for a total of 20 years, and be connected with

Finland for the rest of my life. Finland became home to me more than Britain.

Between my Bible college years I spent the summer in Finland, speaking in some churches under the auspices of the Church of Finland Inland Mission. Two memories remain of that summer.

At their summer conference an Indian missionary was to speak. He had little English but plenty of German, and as they had no-one who was proficient in German I was co-opted to interpret. Everyone thought it was great fun to have an English lady translating a German-speaking Indian into Finnish. - I was less sure about the fun, but managed it somehow. The other thing was that I was beginning to wonder if the Lord wanted me in Finland long-term. Again I asked Him for an answer through an answer. If I asked the Inland Mission director for a place in their work, would God please open or close the door. I asked with trepidation. "Oh yes, I'm sure we have work for you!" was the encouraging answer. The door was flung wide open! This time I didn't doubt, but went back to BTI saying with amazement, "Guess what! The Lord has opened the door for me to work in Finland." Friends were not surprised. "You talk about Finland as if you already belonged there. You say 'we do this' not 'they do this', so we guessed the Lord would have to send you there!!" It is good to consult others or anyway to hear confirmation from others of the way you feel God is leading you.

## Bible College

My two years at the Bible Training Institute (BTI) in Glasgow were challenging and encouraging. I picked up a Glasgow accent, of course, just through living in the city, though staff and students came from all over Britain, and abroad. The building was known as "The grim old castle" and was rather spartan, but the fellowship was warm and welcoming and the teaching excellent. Lectures opened our eyes to the deeper truths of the Bible, and other subjects were to help with ministry. Meanwhile, practical work assignments and living in community gave us the opportunity to put our faith into practice. Practical work could be both hard work and fun, though knocking on doors was difficult for me. However, Glaswegians are so friendly that you were sometimes inside with a cup of tea in your hand before they asked you what you had come for!

Many of the women had given up jobs as nurses or teachers and were living with very little funds. Yet we shared what we had. If one person had received a money gift and knew of another who was in need of something she couldn't afford she would slip a ten-shilling note, or even a pound note into the other girl's Bible or coffee tin whilst she wasn't looking. The giving was always anonymous and was just sharing the Lord's love without causing embarrassment. I both gave and received in this way.

I naturally gravitated towards the European students – Germans and Swiss – and almost became regarded as one of the "foreign students". My closest neighbour and best friend at college was Renée from South Africa. When a young man from South Africa came in our second year we became a threesome. He was Afrikaans-speaking and I was, of course, keen to pick up a bit of that language. I borrowed his Bible and bought a dictionary and composed letters during the holidays. During the Easter break I went with a group to Austria. On the way we stopped over at a Bible college in Belgium, and I was delighted to find I could converse with a girl who spoke Flemish whilst I used Afrikaans. Both languages are similar to Dutch and are close enough to be mutually understandable.

My job in Austria that holiday was to cook for a group of fellows who were renovating an old castle to become a youth centre. I and the German girl who helped me, were not good at cooking German food. One day we were doing sausages and sauerkraut but did it all the wrong way round. Still, the hungry lads ate with gusto.

At the end of the two years we gained our diplomas and parted into many areas of service for Jesus. Some went on to train for ministry in their own denomination, others went out to various mission fields, and some returned to their secular jobs and active lay service within their home church. I was on my way to Finland.

# 4

## BACK IN FINLAND

My first job back in Finland was teaching English and German in a residential college belonging to the Church of Finland Inland Mission. The students were 16-18 yr-olds, mostly girls, who were learning mostly practical skills such as weaving, cooking or woodwork. Another teacher, Pirkko - a girl of my own age - was teaching religious studies there. We got on well and shared in the evangelism outside teaching hours. Apart from organised meetings where we spoke about the Lord, we visited the dormitories in the evenings and chatted with the girls, and arranged testimony meetings round a blazing log fire some Saturdays. Some of the other teachers were against clear evangelism, but others, though not outgoing themselves, rejoiced with us as we shared about the students accepting Jesus as their Saviour one by one.

At the end of that year I had been hoping to move into travelling evangelistic work with the Inland Mission. However, for rather complicated reasons that door closed and the next door that opened was that of Helsinki Bible School. I went for an interview and was told I would replace another English girl if she didn't return from holiday. Finding it involved helping with kindergarten I prayed fervently that she would come back. She didn't. That prayer was not answered the way I wanted, so I had to go ahead with the work. As I had had no experience with young children I was out of my depth, and sat down to cry after my first morning there. But there was no way out and I had to continue. Through it the Lord taught me at least two things: a) to obey Him even when it feels hard (I needed that lesson later!); b) to understand and love small children, and c) learning nursery rhymes and songs in Finnish gave me a deeper knowledge of Finnish background. I later sometimes surprised people by quoting their nursery rhymes. This childhood background and working with Lutherans gave me a "resonance base" to build on even when dealing later with free church people, as they are deep down influenced by the 89% of Lutheranism in the country.

After this time people have sometimes commented how children seem to be at ease with me. "I can see that you love children, and they love you," they will say. I smile. They don't know how hard-won this facility is!

Apart from kindergarten in the mornings I was teaching Bible School students in the afternoons. They were training to become youth leaders, mostly in the Lutheran Church. I started with English but New Testament Greek, World Religions and Piano for Beginners were also added to my curriculum, most of which I enjoyed. I was given a room in the old house used as a hostel for some of the first-year students. The owners, an elderly couple, lived on the upper ground floor, some of our boys lived on the lower ground floor, and the girls and I and an evangelist's family lived upstairs. Nine girls shared two big rooms and I had my own smaller room, which was heated by a wood-burning tiled oven. The problem was, I could only heat it in the morning and evening when I was at home. Consequently it was cosy and warm when I was either out at school or in bed! The family had a bathroom with water heater, but the nine girls and I shared one toilet with washbasin and cold water, and a sitting area with an electric cooking plate. We queued for the toilet, but I took water into my room to save waiting for washing, cooking etc. It stood me in good stead for later years in China to wash in cold water or heat what I needed. When after two years the evangelist's family moved out I took over their living room, boys moved into their bedroom area, which included the bathroom, and we shared the kitchen. Unfortunately the girls' rooms were separated from the kitchen by my room, which consequently became a corridor! A visitor wondered how on earth I could live in this sort of situation, but I was happy to be there living my whole life for Jesus, so it didn't really bother me. And now I had my own tiny washroom, still with cold water, though I still shared the toilet, and continued to visit a friend's home for a bath or sauna.

Life at the school was interesting and enjoyable, though not without its difficulties. The Head, a talented Bible teacher, was not always diplomatic in the office/ staffroom. I was one of the four full-time staff, with other teachers coming in for specific lessons. We four in turn were the brunt of the Head's criticism or irritation, but we supported and encouraged each other and managed to keep smiling. Back at our hostel I was to see the students kept the rules. Not having boys in the girls' rooms after 10pm was the one they most objected to, and I was dubbed an "old maid" by one irate 19-yr old for enforcing it!

## Pirjo

One year we had a spare bed in one of the girls' rooms at the hostel and an outsider was allowed to move in. She was Pirjo, a shy girl from up-country, and she wasn't a Christian. Soon after she arrived I was due to go to an evangelistic weekend camp in central Finland. I invited Pirjo to go with me, and she was very willing. But a couple of days beforehand I went down with a heavy cold and couldn't contemplate travelling. It so happened that just at that time I had to move from my small room into the former family living-room. Pirjo and another friend were helping. We prayed about my health, as it was "tomorrow or not at all". I knew there was a good chance Pirjo might respond to the Gospel there, but she was too shy to go on her own, so I asked the Lord to give her this chance somehow. As we continued with the work the other friend said, "Your eyes look better." They did, and by evening I was just about completely over my feverish cold and could travel next day with Pirjo to the camp.

And yes, Pirjo did realize she needed Jesus there, and at the end of the weekend I was able to help her take the step of asking Jesus to forgive her and come into her life. Of course she then fitted in better with the other girls in our hostel. One discovery she made on her own from reading the Bible was on the question of tithing – giving a tenth of her small income to the Lord, and she turned to me for advice. Previously she had complained that her income was inadequate for her needs. After she had been tithing for some time she came to me with a new "problem". "When I have paid my taxes, rent, food and other necessities," she said, "I still have money left over. How can I use it for the Lord?" What a lovely problem her obedience had caused! She has been actively involved in a local church since this time. Pirjo and I have remained friends through the intervening years. She is not far from having "learning difficulties", but was able to faithfully hold down a routine job until being made redundant and taking early retirement. Although I am at the other end of the intelligence scale we have been able to enrich each other's lives in many ways, and I have enjoyed her hospitality when visiting Helsinki in later years. Above all, we love to remember that whatever our differences Jesus sees us as equals.

## Leena

Another friendship that started at the Bible School was with

Leena, who was "visually challenged" then, and is now almost totally blind. Before coming to Bible School Leena had trained as a masseuse and was happy to practise her skills on her fellow students and me. I appreciated it then and have enjoyed a "working over" many times through the years. She, on the other hand, needed my help as she couldn't read her English textbook. With some effort I managed to master the Braille alphabet, and spent hours writing the books out in Braille for her. When exam time came the other teachers would give me the questions, which I wrote out in Braille, so she could answer them on her ordinary typewriter.

Leena came from a farming family and had learned many household skills despite her impaired vision. In fact she was the one at the hostel who did most of the cleaning in the girls' area. She invited me to her home in summer, where I learned to milk a cow and make hay, both the old-fashioned way. One day a group of us went out to search for the rare and delicious cloudberry. This looks like a blackberry, but is yellow and grows in slightly swampy areas. We found some after wandering a long way in uneven terrain. As I got back to the car I realized I must have twisted my ankle as it began to hurt. Someone else drove my car home with me in the back seat. Arriving back at the farm I could hardly get out of the car as my ankle had stiffened up. Leena's mum had an idea and brought out a small brown bottle of liniment. On her knees she carefully massaged it into my foot for some time, then stopped, sniffed the bottle and started to laugh. It turned out she had two similar bottles and had taken the wrong one, so she had been massaging my ankle with cough mixture! I crawled up to bed and the next morning my ankle was almost completely better. The cough mixture was very effective!

After graduation Leena got a job with the Lutheran Church, helping visually impaired people in Helsinki, socially, spiritually and practically. She has done this ever since, developing the work from small beginnings and being appreciated by those she helps, especially because she is one of them. She married a visually impaired boy and they have brought up two seeing children in a normal family.

The Bible School, like many other churches and institutions, owned a "summer cottage". There was a main building for eating and meetings, several huts for sleeping, and of course a sauna by the lake edge. One summer a busload of German Christian young adults was expected and I was asked to go as their interpreter, since no-one else on the staff spoke German. When the bus arrived I could manage "Guten Tag", but that was about all. My fluent German had been forgotten in the years of Finnish surroundings. I could understand them, of course, but was really ashamed of my stumbling efforts to speak a language I had once been so fluent in. Fortunately the language was there to be rekindled, and it improved day by day as I spent time with the group. Their stay lasted three weeks and in that time not only did my German become fluent again, but I also made lasting friendships.

## Renewed contact with ECM

During my third year at the Bible School I renewed contact with ECM, as one of their directors, Rev. Cecil Young, who was directing the work in France, asked me to arrange some meetings for him. When he spoke at my Bible School I naturally interpreted. It flowed easily as we were on the same wavelength. I was much encouraged when one student commented afterwards, "It was only half-way through the meeting that I realised it was being interpreted." One acquaintance arranged a meeting for us in a Swedish-speaking Free Evangelical church in Helsinki (or Helsingfors, as it is called in Swedish). I felt immediately at home in this informal Monday meeting, despite understanding very little of the language, and determined to visit again later. A few months later I went again and began to be a regular at the Monday meetings, my ears getting attuned to the words and understanding more and more. The people were welcoming and amazed that I could speak fluent Finnish, which most of them could not, although they were Finnish citizens.

I decided some grammar study was needed to get me beyond understanding to speaking, so went to local evening classes twice a week, attending various meetings at the church most other evenings. I was in a small class, which made teaching more effective. About the third lesson the teacher commented on my surname as not being Finnish (people usually asked if I was married to an Englishman) and found I was English. But we had been talking in Finnish and he couldn't understand how any foreigner could speak such perfect Finnish. He tested me with some difficult superlative constructions and when I got them all right he was speechless with amazement. To me it was quite natural after seven years in the country to speak it like a native. So my days ran in Finnish and my evenings in Swedish, and the language learning curve was steep. By the end of one winter I was quite happy speaking at meetings in Swedish. As we had a pastor from Sweden I would always hear the Sweden version of the language from the pulpit, but the Finland version elsewhere. This led to a sub-conscious conviction that one always spoke like a Swede from the pulpit, and as my Swedish improved and I started taking meetings I found myself using two types of intonation, one in the pulpit and one elsewhere. My friends laughed at me, and I could listen to myself doing this, but it was difficult to change. Eventually I managed it, though it sometimes still surfaces when I am nervous.

Having now both languages I was more useful to ECM and after Cecil Young's first visit I began to put out a newsletter in Finnish and Swedish for those who had shown interest in the work. I was now regarded as ECM's official representative, and in this capacity I was invited to their bi-ennial conference, where I felt very much part of the family. The need was expressed for a worker in Scandinavia. I knew I could do the work, having both Finnish and Swedish and knowing the people and the culture. Life at the Bible School was difficult at that point, and I would have been happy to leave. I talked with ECM's General Director, Rev. Stuart Harris, but didn't have complete peace in my heart. Mr. Harris told me to go home and pray about it. This I did, and only got peace when I promised the Lord I would stay on at the school. I obeyed the Lord's red light, even though I was raring to go. The next year turned out to be even more difficult and I felt I was going through a mangle - pressure from above and below. Some six months later a letter from Mr. Harris was God's green light. Now, at the end of this school year I could move into the Mission. At that point the Head was retiring and the incoming Head asked me to stay on. Life will be easier now, he said. But I was no longer running away, but taking a step forward in God's timing, and I had peace.

I will tell more about Finland in the chapter on my ECM years. (ch.9)

Even when I moved away from Finland I continued to visit twice a year and take meetings from my new home in Sweden. But once I moved from Scandinavia my visits were confined mostly to summer holidays, which I would combine with a few meetings. In over 40 years I think there have been only two calendar years when I have not set foot in Finland. It certainly was home to me more than Britain.

The years in Finland were a time of growing and learning. The early years prepared me for the later challenges. Some parts were not at all to my liking, such as work with small children or living with only cold water. But God's criterion is not whether we can handle a big job, but whether we can handle any job or situation well, as we do it all for Him.

There were disappointments and unanswered prayers during those years, and there was much joy in both the work and the life there, and many answered prayers too. Serving the Lord is sometimes fun, though not always, but it is always basically satisfying as we go through the ups and downs of it all. God's lessons develop our character and make us richer and more mature.

## SECTION THREE
### Eastern Europe

# 5

## THE SOVIET UNION

Although at the time I had not yet coined the term "maxi-risk", Eastern Europe in the 1960s and 1970s was certainly a maxi-risk area. The dangers were not only for oneself but also for the contacts made, the local Christians, and great care had to be taken to protect them. I was privileged to be sent by the Lord into several of these countries, where I met precious brothers and sisters who were giving their all to further the work of God, whatever the cost. Could I do less? The blessing of seeing their joy at the encouragement we could bring was indeed worth the maxi-risk. We took Bibles and other literature, clothing, occasionally money, electric equipment, even parts for a printing press once. But our visits, our hugs and encouraging words and prayers, were as much a gift to them as the goods we brought.

## ESTONIA

The European Christian Mission was founded in 1904 in Estonia, whence it spread to other eastern European countries, and later to Western Europe. During my last year at Helsinki Bible School travel to Eastern Europe was becoming a little easier. A boat trip from Helsinki across the Gulf of Finland to Tallinn became possible and I was one of the first to try the route. For some time I had been attending Estonian Bible studies in Helsinki, led by an Estonian-American brother. In this way I had learned to understand some of the language, which is very closely related to Finnish. This brother gave me a booklet to give to the Lutheran archbishop of Estonia. Arriving at the port we went through the customs and I was asked if I had any religious literature. Yes, I answered and produced the booklet, claiming I could take it in as a gift. "I decide that!" snapped the officer and took it away from me, returning it as I left the country two days later. But this rather naive attitude had its benefits. He didn't ask if I had any more literature, so I didn't have to tell about the quantity of gospels and tracts I had strapped round my waist and in pockets all down the back of my loose coat! This was the only time I personally was asked this question, though I made a number of trips. I had obtained the name from ECM of some old contacts of the Mission, and actually once met the widow of one of the original leaders of the Mission. I arranged to meet a lady who was choir leader of a small Baptist Church on the outskirts of Tallinn. We visited their family and also met the pastor of that church and a pastor from another town - Arpád Arder. He was a fearless brother who spoke several languages and kept contact with foreign Christians despite the dangers. These pastors were thrilled when I unloaded my treasures, immediately dividing them into several piles to share amongst the churches.

At church I was asked to bring brief greetings from the West, which I did through Brother Arpád's interpretation from

Finnish. The meeting was closed and we were taken into the back room whilst people went home. After a while we returned to the church to find the members still there, whilst the spies had gone home. They always reckoned on having informers in the open meetings. Then we were asked to tell more openly about Christians in the West, and they shared with us about their situation.

On my second visit I took small New Testaments in. I was met by the children of my choir leader friend, who told me of the sudden death of their father through a stroke. Later I took her a typewriter so she could earn her own living by doing secretarial work. The typewriter, I heard many years later, was still in use, now mainly for the Lord's work. This time I brought greetings in the church in German, as there happened to be an interpreter who spoke German - it is useful to be able to vary one's language according to the interpreter! Before we left the friends asked if we had seen the new Estonian Bible that they had heard about. I had only seen small Bibles and New Testaments but promised to investigate. I had started sending others in with loads of these small Scriptures. But when I found the new Bibles I was horrified to see how big they were - definitely not a smuggling size! I decided I couldn't risk asking others to take these so went again myself. The risky business was now even more "risky". Before this I had been able to spend a month amongst Estonians in Sweden, and had grown from passive understanding of the language to being able to use it myself.

On this trip we lived on the ship and went off as often as we wanted. On first arrival we took nothing through. As we went through customs other times one officer was in his office and a doorman was in the big hall. I tiptoed through the customs, hoping no-one would come out and ask questions, and into the hall, where the doorman was chatting with another official. Under my loose fitting coat I had two of the large Bibles strapped one at the front, one at the back. My friend had gone through first and waited for me outside. On my way though the hall the Bible at my back slipped and fell with a loud thump to the floor. I froze for a second, then with a casual "Oh dear" turned and picked it up, tucked it under my arm and walked out, expecting at every step to be stopped. Nothing. My friend, who had seen it all, said the two men never even turned their heads. From this I know there are angels who make us invisible when the need arises! Brother Arpád was again visiting and he and the other pastor were so thrilled with the new Bibles they couldn't even leave them to come for a meal. When the time came for a word of greeting in church this time I didn't need an interpreter.

Later we made contact with another church and were invited to bring greetings there too - foreigners were not allowed to preach. The friend I was with that time was a Finn who spoke good Estonian. We decided to sing two songs in Estonian. Before we sang the first one I explained why we were singing it and what it meant to us - this took nearly ten minutes. Before the second song my friend did the same. In this way we could testify and share the Lord's love without officially having preached!

As the number of tourists from Finland increased they were noticeable on the streets. Obviously we didn't want to stand out and be followed on our missions to the Christians, so we dressed more shabbily, like the locals. One time we were in the sort of raincoats that were very common in Tallinn. As we came back to the ship the doorman didn't want to let us in. We insisted that we were Finnish tourists and eventually got through, realising with gratitude that if a man expecting tourists didn't recognise us, then we certainly wouldn't stand out in the streets and on the trams.

Returning from a trip in May one year (the boats only ran in the summer season) ice floes were still floating around the Gulf of Finland and we were delayed overnight. This was a blessing for me, as it turned out, but a great disappointment for my students, who had come down to the harbour to welcome me with a 'Welcome' banner written in Estonian but using Greek lettering, (because I taught them Greek!) and with a scruffy piece of red coconut matting from the hall as a welcoming red carpet! As they told me about it afterwards I assured them I would have walked past without acknowledging them. Ah, that wouldn't help, they said, as they would have shouted, "Hello Teacher, we know you!!!" Was I ever grateful for those ice floes!!! The students talked about it for days afterwards and we had good fun.

Years later, other ECM missionaries visited the country and found someone who had kept very old ECM magazines, two of which they were able to bring out, one dating from 1936, the other from a year before or after that. They were precious reminders of the early days of our Mission, but as they were in Estonian I was the only one in the Mission who could read them!

## RUSSIA

### By bus

My first visit to Leningrad (as it was then called) was by coach. I took only two shopping bags. In one I had a false bottom with a few Bibles underneath, and all my clothes on top. In the other I had all Bibles covered only with a cardigan. When we arrived at the border we were ordered to take our bags to the customs shed. The officer came along the line. My heart was pounding and my soul was praying hard. Stopping in front of me he put his hand down the side of one bag to see if there was a false bottom. There wasn't. Then he looked in the top of the other one and found clothing. He nodded approval and moved on to the next. Little did he realise what he would have found if he had inspected those bags the other way round.... Thank you, Lord! Through the friends I travelled with I was introduced to a Finnish-speaking Russian sister. Following her to her home was quite an adventure as we tried to look as Russian as possible and mingle with the crowd, whilst following her from a distance. Wearing a western style hat I went down the underpass to cross under the busy main road. Coming up the other side I was wearing a Russian-looking headscarf! This sister knew how to pass on the Bibles to others further away from western contacts.

## By boat

The second time I visited her I was trying out a new route with my sister. A boat travelled from a Finnish inland port down the beautiful Saimaa Canal and then across the Gulf of Finland to Leningrad. As in Tallinn, we lived on the boat and went into the city as and when we wanted, only waving our passports at the sailor on duty at the gangway. We couldn't wear coats in the summer weather, but had loose-fitting dresses of sturdy material, which could cover literature strapped around out waists. One time we even asked the sailor on duty to take a photo of us - good job it wasn't an x-ray camera!! We visited the sister one day and met a brother who had come from far out east looking for Bibles and a tape-recorder to use in the church's work. This was the Lord's perfect timing, bringing us together with the right help at the right time. He got our Bibles and I said that we had a tape-recorder on board the ship. Plans were made and we returned to the ship for a rest. As dusk was falling we set off again for the park near where the ship was berthed. I had a common kind of Finnish shopping bag containing the tape-recorder. We wandered into the almost deserted park and as arranged passed the brother sitting on a bench reading a newspaper. Beside him was an identical shopping bag to mine. We took no notice of him. A moment later I heard footsteps approaching from behind. He walked smartly past us, but at the crucial moment we swapped bags. My bag now contained a newspaper, his the tape-recorder. What joy there would be back in his church, when they could record the services and take them out to the sick and elderly. It was all worth the risk, for him and for us. And although it was a real risk for him, it was still quite fun swapping bags in a one-second walk-past in a Leningrad park in the gathering dusk!

## By car

Getting into Russia wasn't always easy, even though the growing number of welcome tourists made checks somewhat lighter. One time it all went wrong. By this time I had moved into ECM work and was travelling with a colleague, who had been taking meetings in Scandinavia, to a conference in Italy, planning to pass through the Soviet Union. We followed her method, used in other Eastern European countries, of putting most of the Bibles in one case and praying we wouldn't have to open that one. For the Soviet Union it didn't work. They had almost passed us, not finding anything, when one Bible, not in the case, was found. The whole car was searched more thoroughly and the caseful discovered. Now we were in trouble, and yet the Lord gave us a serenity that kept us through the tense moments. I stood in the main hall praying and feeling the Lord's comfort. When I opened my eyes a group of border guards was standing staring at me. They had probably never seen anyone praying. We were taken into a room with two women who searched us and found some small scriptures on our person. We put them into a pile. Thinking it was now finished one lady slipped out and I had the chance in a few seconds to ask the other lady if she believed in God. She nodded. Would she like a John's gospel? She put her finger to her lips and then drew it across her throat. I understood and quickly passed her a copy, which she slipped into her pocket just as the door opened and the other lady returned. We were separated and questioned, found later our answers had not contradicted each other.

As the car was mine I was the main culprit and was cross-examined by a Finnish-speaking officer. Although such interviews should never be conducted by one man - they don't trust each other - during my interview other officers came and went. Whenever we were alone the man asked me about my faith and I found his grandfather had been a Christian. I explained our love for Russian Christians and our desire to help them, and challenged him on his need of the Saviour. Eventually, because he couldn't get any information from me about where the literature had come from, he passed me over to an English-speaking officer. I gave him a simple reason for what we were doing - that God loves everybody and there are Christians in the Soviet Union who need Bibles. The second man was less responsive, but still didn't get the information he wanted. Eventually we were re-united and left to wait for the return of our passports with cancelled visas. Meanwhile the lady who had searched us came to talk - we were in the hall with officers playing chess at the other end. Whilst we seemingly admired some souvenirs we had bought we talked quietly in German about the Lord with this dear soul, who was not a customs officer but only a Ministry of Agriculture employee. I believe the little faith she had was strengthened by our visit and testimony.

Eventually the passports were returned and a young officer escorted us to the car. He asked in Russian why we had done this. My Russian was very limited and I could only reply that when Jesus is in the heart we have peace. We returned to Helsinki and took another route to the conference. It had all gone wrong - or had it? Customs men often slip confiscated Bibles into their pockets, some are sold on the black market, and some read them themselves. And I had been able to witness in four languages to four people who may not otherwise have heard of God's love for them. So maybe it didn't all go wrong after all.

# 6

## POLAND

At some point I had been given the name and address of a lady in Poland known to ECM. A brother in Germany had given me the name of a contact at Warsaw Baptist Church. But when I felt I should make a trip to Poland I could find none of this information. Thus it was that a Finnish friend and I set off with a load of Russian Bibles and children's clothing but with no contacts to take them to. Maxi-risk again! Some friends in Sweden had acquired the Russian Bibles for us, but wisely didn't ask which country we were going to. They said they had just had some Hungarian New Testaments returned, which they had tried to send to that country by post. I wasn't going to Hungary so couldn't help. But as they were about to wave us off, I had a sudden urge to take the packet, and sent the daughter to fetch it, pushing it under my seat and almost forgetting it.

We arrived at a Polish port with an unpronounceable name and sat in line at the customs. The car in front of us was emptied and all corners dug into. They were very thorough. We watched in horror and prayed that we wouldn't have that treatment. When the officer came to us he checked our papers and asked if we had any presents. I didn't answer that question but pointed to the borrowed tent on our roof rack, smiled and said "Camping". He nodded and waved us through. Unbelievable! Our wheels hardly touched the ground for the next ten kilometres, and when we stopped for breakfast in a field the skylarks sang their beautiful song of praise to the Lord as our hearts sang to thank Him for that amazingly easy entry.

We pushed on with no destination in mind, vaguely making for a place where there was a big camping place. As we arrived at the campsite I spotted two Scandinavian cars and decided to stop in that corner. Once the tent was up I went and chatted to our neighbours. The Dane puffed away at his cigarette as he told me where they had travelled. The Swede had a guitar in his hand as we chatted. Later I wondered if he was a Christian, though of course the guitar was no guarantee of that. I couldn't just go and ask, so next morning I sat in our tent and sang some Christian songs in Swedish - just loud enough to be heard next door. Then I took some pots to the kitchen to wash. The Swedish lad came in also with a pan and we chatted again. He mentioned that he had heard me singing. I sounded surprised - "Could you hear it that far away? Well did you know the songs?" "Yes," he said, "at least the one 'I have decided to follow Jesus'." Click - there was the contact and we could chat about missions we both knew. Without saying anything specific we both knew what sort of mission we were on. I said we had no addresses and he turned up with a book giving the addresses of all Baptist churches in Europe. I noted the Warsaw church address and one or two others, in case we went that way. The Lord was leading us step by step, just enough light for the next move.

We had packed food for the journey in my little Volkswagen "beetle" and stopped just off the road one day for a meal. As we delved into the boot at the front a police car drove past. We hoped he had not noticed us, but a couple of minutes later he returned. Oh dear, now what? We had no common language to communicate with the friendly-looking policeman, but soon realised he was offering to help. He was not familiar with "beetles" which have the engine at the back, and thought he had seen two ladies with an engine problem. When he understood the situation he drove off, with our thanks for his kindness, and we continued our meal with great relief.

We drove towards Warsaw. But it is big city and a small road is hard to find, and one doesn't like to ask for a Christian church in a communist country. As we approached the city it started to rain - nay - pour. No point in stopping in this downpour, so I 'followed my nose' and kept driving, with a prayer in my heart. As soon as the rain stopped I stopped and asked the nearest person for directions to the street I was looking for. Amazingly his answer was "First right and first right again, and you are there." I could hardly believe it. God had used the rain - and perhaps an angel's hand on the steering wheel - to guide us to our destination! At the church, still not knowing the name of the contact I was looking for I gave the name of my contact in Germany and the link was soon made. He was very glad to take half our load of Scriptures and clothing. I don't remember who we eventually gave the rest to. There was a youth conference going on at the church, with young people from around the country. I was asked to speak to them, which I did. My friend spoke only Finnish and was happy to help with the driving and be praying in the background whilst I did the communicating in whatever language.

Two girls from a town in the east asked if we would go home with them the next day. Meanwhile they wanted to visit a lady in Warsaw and took us with them. As we walked in and were introduced the lady praised God for answered prayer - she wanted to send out important letters to the West and had prayed for visitors to take them. When I heard her name I realised this was the ECM contact I had been given but lost. God doesn't lose addresses and took us to her anyway! As we chatted I felt the urge to ask about Hungary,

"Do you have any contact with Hungary?"

"Yes," she answered cautiously, "a little. Why?"

"Oh, nothing really," I replied equally cautiously, "it's just that I have a few New Testaments in Hungarian with me." The words were hardly out of my mouth and the dear sister was jumping for joy again.

"Praise the Lord! Praise the Lord! We have visitors coming from Hungary tomorrow and I had prayed God would give me something for them to take back."

Wow! God is very exact, isn't He! I love being the answer to other people's prayers. It gives me a shiver of joy to know He is leading as I walk prayerfully before Him and obey the urges He gives.

We took the girls home next day and 'bush telegraph' got the message round that there would be a youth meeting that evening. A good number turned up. I didn't know what to talk on, but flicking through a small notebook I found a few notes taken from a sermon on the Holy Spirit. I used these as the basis of my talk on how to experience the fullness of God's Spirit. Afterwards the girls said they had had so little teaching on the Holy Spirit, this was just what they needed. Bull's eye again, Lord!

Another girl at the conference had given us the address of her relatives in another town, and as we were going that way we called. But her message to them had not got through, they had no warning of our arrival. Nevertheless they opened their hearts and home to sisters from the West, gave us their bed whilst they made do on a sofa. It was very moving and a testimony to their living in Jesus' love. At the next town, Gdansk, we found the church, but only the pastor's wife at home. It turned out she was German-speaking so no difficulties in communication. (This part of Prussia had been taken over by Poland after WW2 and many still speak German.) Would we bring greetings at the meeting that night? Of course, we would love to. They hadn't got anyone who could translate from English, so a German-speaking interpreter was found and I spoke to the meeting through her. I noticed two older ladies having a little weep, and wondered what I had said that moved them. When I went to talk to them I found it was the language I had used. "We are originally German," they said, "and we have learnt Polish, married Poles. But to hear God's Word in our mother tongue - oh, it was so wonderful!"

Now I wonder why they couldn't find an English interpreter...........!

When we arrived back at the point of entry for our return journey we could hardly believe we had lived through such a week. Entering with no names or addresses we had been able to give away all the Scriptures and clothing we had, had visited nine homes and spoken in three churches, and been God's answer to other people's prayers. It was indeed a week to remember, and to praise God for.

# 7

## ROMANIA

This time we set off from Vienna - Barbara, a seasoned traveller in the east, and myself. We spent New Year in Hungary and approached the Romanian border, trying to sing choruses on the way. But only one would come out - "He is Lord....every knee shall bow, every tongue confess that Jesus Christ is Lord." However hard we tried to think of other choruses this was the only one we could sing, over and over again. We felt we were going through a spiritual battle as we drove towards the border. The border was reached with pounding hearts and an official came out, ordering the boot to be opened. I sat in the car whilst Barbara did the talking. She had warned me he would want me out of the car so he could look in the glove compartment. She opened a case for him - not the one with the Bibles in, and then he asked her if she had any weapons. A definite No to that (not counting the Sword of the Spirit, of course) and then he asked, "Have you any Bibles?" "Any what?" replied my canny colleague.

"Holy books, holy books," he continued, at which Barbara looked blank and asked what he meant. "Never mind. Where are you going?" were his next words and she suggested we might aim for the Black Sea coast. "To swim?" he asked, and they both laughed, as it was January. Giving me hardly a glance he waved the two stupid women on their way. Suddenly we were singing all sorts of choruses - the lion had been bound by the declaration that He is Lord, and now we were free to sing praises. We had entered the lion's mouth and found he had no teeth!

Our journey had brought us through Hungary and Christians there, knowing we were continuing to Romania, gave us gifts of food, including some large white crusty loaves of bread. When we arrived in one Romanian home we put a large loaf on the kitchen table, and then went in to see the father, who was dying of cancer. As we sat with him members of the family came and went, unable to resist the temptation of the white bread as they passed. By the time we departed only half of it was left – but that was just why we brought it, we knew it was a rare delicacy for them.

In another family the sons had just been able to get another rare delicacy – some meat fat, but with no meat. They offered this to us, but we declined, partly because it didn't appeal to us, but mostly because we wouldn't take this delicacy from them. The mother had a bad arm and I asked why she didn't go to the doctor. She replied that they couldn't afford it. I was amazed, and said I thought medical care was free in communist countries. Ah yes, in theory, but she explained that doctors would not see patients who didn't bring a sizeable bribe, and these Christians could not afford one. This was my first experience of the corruption in this system. The husband was known as an active Christian and was therefore given a double work shift to keep him from having time for such activities. The money, however, was not doubled.

At one church we visited we were impressed in the open time of prayer to hear these dear souls pouring out their hearts to God, who carried them through all the difficulties they had to face in that country. In northern Romania we found Romanian, Hungarian and German congregations sharing the same church, even worshipping together with interpretation. We were able to give Bibles to Christians already known to us, but forgot to give away the Russian-made radio we had brought from Vienna. One of our missions on that trip was to pass on roubles to be smuggled through to help families of Christian prisoners in the neighbouring Soviet Union. This was real risky business! Friends in Brasov couldn't help us, but suggested an old brother in another town and gave us his address.

We found the town, the street and house, but parked further away so as not to draw attention to the fact that westerners were visiting him. As we got out of the car Barbara suggested I put the radio and last two Bibles in my bag. Brother Tom gave us a warm welcome. He spoke good English, having been in prison for translating Christian books into Romanian. We sat and talked for some time. Then I asked if he listened to the Romanian Christian radio broadcasts from Monte Carlo. We knew that many listened and found these broadcasts a real lifeline. He smiled and said he had given his radio away 12 years ago and never been able to buy one since, but he knew many people listened and loved them. Would he listen if he had a radio? - I asked. Well, he said, his older sister who lived with him was losing her sight so it was difficult for her to go to church. (Romanian roads and pavements are terrible even for those with good eyesight!) But, he shrugged, he had no way to be able to buy a radio. By this time I was reaching into my bag and produced the radio, putting it on the table in front of him. "Now you have one," I said quietly. His face went very serious, almost shocked, as he stared at the radio. "It's a miracle," he whispered. Then louder, "It's a miracle!" Looking up at us he said "No-one, not even my sister, knows that I started praying for a radio just two days ago. I have never had such a quick answer to prayer." At that moment his sister came into the room and he showed her the radio. She saw the two books I had also put on the table, and feeling them recognised them as Bibles. "Oh, how lovely!" she exclaimed. "Yesterday we gave away the last of the extra Bibles we had and today the Lord has sent us two more." We were all very moved. God had been so good to these faithful servants, and he had done it through other servants who had no idea of their needs but who followed the Lord's nudges.

However, Brother Tom could not help us with the roubles, but gave us a further address on the border with the Soviet Union. We set off again - the risk was getting even more "maxi" as this was an area not frequented by westerners. We prayed for good weather so we could travel quickly and safely. But soon it started to snow quite heavily. Oh dear, Lord, we didn't ask for this! As we passed through a town a few people were trudging along with their collars turned up and their eyes on their feet. I didn't check, but I imagine our numberplate was soon unreadable and no-one was noticing a foreign car slipping through the town. God had better ideas than we had. Reaching the next town we soon found the address. It was late and the people had gone to bed, but welcomed us warmly nevertheless. Before we talked business we all stood and praised the Lord for a safe journey there, and asked for further protection for us all. Yes these people had contacts over the border and would deliver the roubles safely. Our visit was short and we slipped out into the night. We had parked behind a hedge, and as we sat in the car, before starting the engine we saw a police car arrive in the town, passing just the other side of the hedge. As they went one way we went the other, and there was no trail to see where we had been!

Petrol was getting alarmingly low. On the way up I had argued that we would draw too much attention to ourselves if we stopped for petrol, but now we were risking getting stranded. We tried to stop for some sleep, but it was cold in the mountains and we dared not leave the motor running. Our little butane gas cooker helped, but we eventually had to move on. We came to a

little town as dawn began to break. Seeing a petrol station
Barbara said we would have to sit there until they opened, as she
didn't dare drive further. I had laughed at the thought there
might be stations that were open overnight - be glad there are
some that are open in daytime, I had said. But as we turned off
the engine an old man appeared, rubbing the sleep from his eyes
and filled up our tank. He took our money but was too sleepy to
ask questions! And so, once out in the country again, we could
stop for some sleep with the engine running to keep us warm.
(Forget the pollution, please, it was a maxi-risk situation!) We
had to cross some mountains where a sign warned that tyres
needed to have snow chains, which we didn't have. The pine and
fir trees rose majestically on every side, their branches weighed
down with snow. The snow had been ploughed and stood
banked high on both sides as we passed through. I prayed as I
drove up the steep and winding roads, "Lord, don't let us get
stuck!" And He didn't. At one point we came across some
soldiers trying to get their van out of the ditch. Rather than
wonder what we were doing there they seemed embarrassed to
be holding us up and soon hopped in and shot off. How grateful
I was that the Lord kept us out of the ditch. We arrived at the
next bigger town, booked into a hotel room and slept all
morning after our day and night of adventure. Maxi-risk can be
tiring! But it was worth it when I think of the joy and blessing we
had been to God's children under pressure, including those
whose men were in prison for Christ's sake.

On the way home we drove through Yugoslavia, as we
wanted to visit a friend there. It was difficult to find up in the
mountains, but eventually we arrived and sat and talked for
several hours. It was a difficult conversation because of the
subject. By the time we turned in for the night we were frozen,
at least from the knees down, as we were in a draughty
farmhouse in January. We were to sleep in an outhouse, a small
room with two beds and a small stove. Despite putting on more
clothes than we took off we could not sleep, and even nibbled

peanuts at 3am. Eventually, because of the cold we decided we needed to warm each other. Barbara crept into my bed, and lying back to back gave just the warmth that got us to sleep immediately. Waking an hour later I didn't dare move for fear of disturbing Barbara, and lay uncomfortable the rest of the night. In the morning I had a painful cramp in my stomach – result of the cold and stress of the evening and night on top of the long stressful journey with poor food. Barbara usually carried a mini-flask of cognac for such disorders but had run out. As soon as we crossed into Austria we stopped and bought some, which, like the good nurse she was, she dosed me with in a mug of hot sweet water. It helped and we got safely back to Vienna, but it took a few days of rest and good food to completely restore me. Risky business is costly, but Jesus said we should take up our cross and follow Him. Tiredness and discomfort in His service are all part of our cross. At one point on the trip when we were absolutely exhausted, Barbara and I smiled at each other and said, "Isn't it good to be tired for Jesus!"

# 8

## HUNGARY

When I later lived in Hungary I found the atmosphere very different from my earlier visits to the country under communist regime. A Christian teacher told us that the pressure on her was subtle but strong. Having a nose – or rather an ear - for language I quickly picked out a few words that sounded like Finnish. It is grammatically closely related to Finnish, but the vocabulary is mostly unrecognisable, having been influenced by different sources. However, a few basic words can be found:

kéz/käsi (hand);

víz/vesi (water);

vér/veri (blood);

él/elää (he lives);

hál/kala (fish).

What wonderful words to make a sermon out of! I spoke through translation on these words to a group of Christians and they were fascinated, calling the Finns their cousins. I am sure the message was more memorable for them because of that context.

As we continued our journey we stayed with Christians who were so grateful for the goods we had brought them. The table, as always in Eastern Europe, was laden with food, even though they didn't have much for themselves, and our car was lovingly washed before we set off again. Someone suggested we should visit a brother living near the Soviet border, who worked amongst the many gypsies there. They live in villages in very poor conditions and are, not without reason usually, looked down on by the more law-abiding Hungarians. So we set off for the town, with rough instructions how to find this brother's shop - he was a grocer. On the way my companion, Barbara, declared that there are three international words - Hallelujah, Amen, and Coca-cola!! The shop was easy to spot and we went in. A lady and young girl were behind the counter and I could only say his name with a question mark in my voice. The lady shook her head, but somehow we felt we should still hang around. She served the other customers, then, when we were alone she came round and stood in front of us "Hallelujah??" she asked. "Hallelujah!!" I replied, and it was hugs all round. Now this dear sister turned round and pointing to some bottles asked "Coca-cola?" "Amen!" we agreed!! Soon Brother Jenö appeared, the shop was shut and we went home with them for lunch. In fact we stayed over the weekend - what a weekend. With his few words of German and English and my few words of Hungarian and Russian, plus gestures, drawings and lots of Hallelujahs we had a hilarious couple of days. Barbara was a nurse and saw the illnesses affecting the people we met. I was the communicator who could pass on her recommendations for treatment. We were a good team.

This dear brother told us with a few words and lots of gestures how he had come to start this ministry, and it is difficult to reproduce his account on paper. He had asked the Lord for direction. "Where to, Lord?" "Gypsies," the Lord replied. But

Jenö was shocked. "No no, Lord, I am a respectable shopkeeper and they are dirty. They smell." So he left it, but some time later again asked, "Where to, Lord?" Again the Lord replied that he was to go to the gypsies, but this time - and here Jenö made a gesture of pouring a jug of water over his head - the Lord filled him with the Holy Spirit. "Ah," he said, rubbing his heart to show the warmth, then spread out his hands with joy, "Gypsies!" So he went to the gypsy villages, sat on the floor with them and didn't even notice the smell. (We did when we went into their houses!!) He pointed to an imaginary book in his hand - "Jesus!" he said. "Jesus?" they replied. He closed his eyes, then opened them slowly. "Jesus? Jesus? Ah, Jesus!" And so graphically he showed how their eyes had been opened to know the Saviour through his testimony.

On New Year's Eve Brother Jenö took us to a gypsy village right on the Soviet border. Our car was hidden, curtains were tightly drawn and bush telegraph gathered a roomful of people, about 40, squashed like sardines into a room with a bed, table and wardrobe. Some young people sat on top of the wardrobe, most stood through the meeting, which lasted a couple of hours. They sang their hearts out, we sang to them, with gestures to help the meaning, they prayed with many cries of "Drága Jézus" (Precious Jesus), and Brother Jenö preached. Something inside me was urging me to speak about suffering. I couldn't understand it.

- "I've got to say something," I whispered to Barbara.
- "Well say it!" was her helpful reply.

But how? A Bible text came into my mind, which I looked up in the German NT I had with me. I showed it to Brother Jenö and he read it in Hungarian. Then, using the few words I knew, a few grammatical endings I had picked up, and the words from the text I managed to speak on the need to be ready to suffer for Jesus as well as rejoice in Him. Jenö listened carefully, caught my meaning and translated it into proper Hungarian. I listened carefully and understood that he had interpreted correctly.

When I had finished I sighed with relief, still not knowing why I had to say this. It was only six months later, when Barbara had further news from there, which said the gypsies had been so open and bold in their faith that they had come under persecution. But God had prepared them through someone who neither knew the future nor spoke their language. God is absolutely amazing - He let a donkey speak in the OT and an almost equally 'dumb animal' in this situation. All Glory to Him!

In 1982 I had the possibility to study Hungarian for a month at the summer university in Debrecen, Hungary's second city. I attended the near-beginners' class in Finnish, as grammatically it is easier to move from that language to Hungarian than from English or German. There were classes at various levels and in various languages. Most of the students were there for the holiday and spent all their free time sunbathing by the lake. My teacher soon found that I was different, as I really wanted to learn – a great encouragement for a teacher, as I know. So instead of spending my afternoons by the lake I was often having extra lessons from her, because I was behind the rest of the class, who had studied in Finland. My evenings were not spent at parties, but often at a local church, where I learned more of the language and enjoyed warm fellowship. I visited Jenö's family and heard that the gypsy work was now in gypsy hands, they even had their own gypsy pastor. The faithful shopkeeper's work was bearing rich fruit.

A few years later I arrived with another colleague in Debrecen and heard that Jenö and family had moved there. Moreover it was his elder daughter's wedding that weekend. We contacted the family at their home, and then I walked along to his new shop. He had no idea I was coming. I stood outside the shop looking at the vegetables, as I saw he had a customer. I was planning to walk in and ask for something, and see if there would be a glimmer of recognition – in Hungary I didn't look at all foreign. But he saw me through the window, left the customer standing open-mouthed and rushed out to hug me shouting

"Paula! Paula!" Of course we stayed for the wedding, which was most interesting and took all day. There were photographs, the official wedding at the registry office - very tastefully done - a meal for invited guests, a church service to bless the marriage, with testimonies, and a buffet meal for all. Brother Jenö is now in the presence of his Lord.

The TWR Christian radio broadcasts from Monte Carlo were much appreciated also in Hungary. One pastor had been allowed out to attend an autumn conference in Switzerland. There he had been given a radio-cassette player, which delighted him, but posed a problem. Hungarians were not allowed to take electrical equipment back from abroad. So he left it with us - I was living in southern Germany at the time - in the hope somebody could take it in to him sometime. It wasn't easy for foreigners to take such things in either. It so happened that I had started to study Hungarian at that time, with the idea of being less helpless on future visits to that country. It also interested me because of its grammatical similarity to Finnish. I had obtained a book and taken some lessons from a Hungarian-speaking Romanian lady living near me. I asked her to record some sentences on cassette so I could listen and practise at home. When it was suggested in December that I might go on a trip to Hungary I was given the radio to take in. But how do I get it through the customs? I hit on the idea of taking my Hungarian book along, and put my tape into the cassette recorder.

When I arrived at the border a young officer asked me if I had any electrical equipment. Yes, I had. I opened the boot, took out the book and cassette recorder and showed him - "I am learning Hungarian," I said in Hungarian. "Play it!" he ordered, so I pressed the 'play' button. Hungarian words came out, slowly and clearly. He now believed me, motioned to stop it and waved me through. When we found the home of the pastor he was both surprised and delighted that he received his gift so soon - just in time for Christmas. Playing Father Christmas is great in such situations, not giving expensive and unnecessary gifts to those who already have so much, but bringing precious gifts that will be a blessing to those who have so little!

These chapters on Eastern Europe read like an exciting series of adventures, and looking back it is fun to recount them. But I am not one who goes into adventure for the sake of it. And at the time, the adventures sometimes felt very uncomfortable, even scary. But these adventures should only be undertaken at God's instigation. I met a lady who had taken one NT with her to Estonia. It was found by the customs men and taken away. She came home saying - "I knew they'd find it!" My comment was that she should never have taken it with that attitude, and without the Lord's permission. It is safe to go into an adventure where Jesus is going ahead.

## SECTION FOUR
### Eighteen Years with the European Christian Mission

# 9

## BEGINNING IN FINLAND

At last, after nine good years, the last of the predictions the Lord had given me at Easter 1960 fitted into place as I left the Bible School and moved into ECM work in June 1969. I had, of course, to leave the hostel that belonged to the Bible School. We found a house outside Helsinki, which we initially shared with another mission, but eventually took over completely. Apart from a few months I always had others living there too. Friends who were temporarily homeless, a couple just arrived from England, students, a young working couple, a girl from England (who made me realize how much English I had forgotten), a short-term co-worker, - the three bedrooms, and sometimes the dividable living room, were rarely empty. It was good to share, and of course it helped the finances.

I had to build up contacts with churches throughout Finland, produce a regular newsletter and take meetings to tell about Europe as a mission field. Going to new places and standing up before unknown people was a bit daunting. As I was introduced as English they were amazed to hear me speaking like a native, and I guessed the first few minutes would be taken up getting over that shock. So I developed a habit of taking a few minutes of introduction. A gentle joke could break the ice, and then a song would give them time to get used to me, so I carried my guitar with me, and a supply of songs. Then, once they had realized I was human after all, I could get down to the message, by which time the people could take it in. But in the late 1960s bringing the message of Europe was no easy task. Finland was acknowledged as not all Christian, the rest of the world was seen as a mission field, but Catholic Europe, oh, they are all Christians there! Needless to say, there was no knowledge of the Catholicism found in southern Europe. Many have now forgotten that until 1967 or '68 it was forbidden for Catholics to read the Bible for themselves. In Britain the Protestant influence helped them to know it to some extent, but in Catholic countries the ignorance of the people about the Bible was (and often still is) total.

The other problem was that ECM is a para-church mission, whereas Finland was locked into its denominations. A mission that was not exclusively their denomination was deeply suspect. It was like banging my head against not one but two brick walls. But with a head like mine, together with a Lord like mine, it was the walls that had to give way!! One by one the doors opened for me to speak, usually through one contact to another. After I had been the first time there was always a warm invitation to come again, as they appreciated the Word of God and the information, even though they didn't necessarily want to get involved. And gradually eyes were opened. There were one or two other people around the same time in Scandinavia and Finland, who were also insisting that Europe needed the Gospel, and as God used all of us, people began to accept the truth of this. Although no candidates eventually were sent out through ECM there are today a number of Finns and Scandinavians working in Europe, some challenged and called through my meetings, for which I praise the Lord. Others were challenged to mission and went out to other parts of the world.

## FMF – the Swedish-speaking Evangelical Free Church

After attending for some time I became a member of the Swedish-speaking Free Evangelical Church in Finland, FMF, who at that time had just three missionaries in Taiwan - a remnant of the days they had sent missionaries to China. As I talked of Europe they thought I was somewhat crazy, as China was the only field they had vision for. But I had a very Finnish quality - sisu - which roughly means "stickability" and I didn't give up easily. God led me to contact with one evangelist/pastor within the church, who was seeking the Lord's direction for his missionary vision. Just at that time I phoned to ask if he would join the new ECM committee for Finland. You can catch fish one by one, but if you catch a fisherman he will catch the fish for you! Kai was that fisherman. Known and respected throughout the small denomination, when he came on board people listened to him. I sent him on a visit to some of our missionaries on the Continent, and this opened his eyes to the spiritual darkness there. When he arrived in one town in France the missionaries were so despondent that they were about to give up and go home. Kai encouraged them to hang in there, which they did. Today the church in that town is flourishing - as much as a church can in France.

As Kai spoke and the people in Finland understood, they too began to get the vision. Through other contacts they had, they began to reach out to other countries - Ecuador was first, and support of ECM's Albanian radio-evangelist was next. It didn't stop there, they later supported me right up to my retirement, and other countries came into the picture as God called the young people to various parts of the world. In fact the missionary vision of FMF mushroomed out of all proportion to the number of members. They even sent two pensioner couples to share their expertise and Christ's love with the people in Ecuador. The moderator of the denomination said to me years later, "When you first came and spoke about Europe we thought you were quite wrong and a bit strange. But you didn't give up and gradually our eyes were opened to see the truth."

Did you know that God has a sense of humour? When I had weaned my church folk away from thinking only of China, and they had turned the whole world into their mission field, I came back and told them God was sending me to China, not Taiwan, but Mainland China, where their missionary work had started many, many years ago!!! Were they pleased? Guess! But that is jumping too far ahead.

Even though my meetings didn't produce many missionaries for Europe, and none through ECM, the Lord could use me to spread blessing in many places as I taught Bible truths in the churches. I became friendly with a Lutheran deaconess (like a church district nurse) in a small village where I had taken a missionary meeting. One time I was visiting her the choirmaster/organist came to say the choir needed help in the altos for their traditional Good Friday concert, and would I help? (I often sang at my meetings, so he had heard that I have quite a decent mezzo-soprano voice.) Of course I would, and arranged to come over for the next practice. When I arrived the choirmaster presented me with two solos he wanted me to sing and a duet he wanted me to sing with a local teacher in addition to the choir pieces. Then the vicar heard I would be singing that day and said: "We always have a visiting speaker at the meeting, so if Pauline is here she can speak." So it was a busy day, with only time to run from the choir balcony to the pulpit and back. But a year later one old lady told the deaconess what I had spoken on, so it had been well remembered.

It wasn't all ministry and I visited this deaconess once to go skiing with her. At the end of the first day we were so exhausted that we had to make coffee to wake us up enough to go to bed!

Although I never became really proficient at skiing it was a good way to enjoy "the great outdoors" in winter.

I arrived at another small town for a meeting agreed with the pastor when I had met him at a pastors' conference. The church was dark and no-one was at home in the pastor's flat. I had the address of the chairman of the deacons and went there. I found the deacons and a very embarrassed pastor having a meeting. The pastor had written down the date in one diary but not transferred it to his church diary. I chatted with the men and told them more about Europe and ECM, which meant they became more interested and when I visited at a later date the welcome was all the warmer.

At one time, when I didn't have a car, I was able to borrow one to take a visiting missionary round to meetings. What I didn't know was that the petrol gauge was faulty and we ran out of petrol on the way to one meeting. Fortunately we had left in very good time, so when we eventually arrived after obtaining petrol with the help of a passing motorist, we were only a few minutes late. There were no mobile phones in those days, so I couldn't let the folk know what had happened. I expected the congregation would sing to pass the time waiting for us, but they are very quiet people in that area. As we opened the outer church door it was deadly quiet and empty. Maybe they had all gone home. I cautiously opened the door into the main hall and saw the congregation sitting in absolute silence, not a cough, not a murmur. We went in and explained to rather stony faces about our predicament, and then went ahead with the meeting. It felt chilly and I couldn't warm them up in the first part of the meeting. But once Jill, who worked in a children's home in France, started telling about her work they began to warm up. It seems they were themselves keen on children's work and by the end of the meeting there was real enthusiasm and friendliness.

Jill and I went on to another meeting, where the congregation were from both Finnish and Swedish speaking groups so I had to interpret her English into both. I don't know how I did it, and wouldn't choose to do it again, but it ran well and all appreciated the message in their language. Although I am happy to converse in a number of languages I don't really like interpreting. Yet I have been called on to do it in the most diverse combinations such as Estonian<->Swedish; Hungarian<->Chinese; German<->Finnish, quite apart from combinations to and from English. It has been challenging but gave a sense of achievement afterwards.

Another memorable occasion was when I was giving a Bible study on Nehemiah at a Youth Weekend in one town. It was on Friday evening, and I planned to go into the forest on Saturday to pick the delicious red berries that were in season. But the young people wanted more of the Bible study on Saturday morning. When I was asked to continue I thought of the berries I was looking forward to taking back to Helsinki to preserve for the winter months, but decided there was no competition - the ministry was more important. We had the study on Saturday, and then to my surprise everybody grabbed a bucket or bowl and sprang out into the forest. In only a short time I had more berries than I would have picked in the whole morning by myself. It was a wonderful reward for putting God's work and others first.

As the above example shows, I didn't talk only on mission, but preached the Word. At one church the pastor stood up at the end and told the congregation I had only arrived half an hour before the meeting – just time for a cup of coffee. I was mystified. Why did he say that? When I asked him he explained that I had spoken so exactly into their situation and needs that the people would think he had told me all the church's problems. No, it was just the Holy Spirit directing my preparation to the right message without any foreknowledge of their situation. Praise the Lord! This happened more than once.

I often had slides and a projector with me on my travels, but during the time I was without a car I asked the churches to provide a projector. One time the projector was set up and then the bulb blew and they didn't have a spare. Catastrophe. I thought quickly and then used word pictures, asking the people to close their eyes and imagine the picture I was drawing for them. It proved most effective, folk said they preferred it to seeing slides as they could use their imagination and it put feeling into the pictures and situations. Necessity is the mother of invention!

*With Grandma, Mum and my sisters on holiday on the beach.*
*(Dad took the photo)*

*I had my 17th birthday in Germany during my first visit*
*abroad.*

*I graduated in 1960, but God had already changed the direction of
my life from an academic to a more practical direction.*

*Anna-Maija, Leena and my mother by the lakeside. My parents visited me in Finland after my first year there.*

*With my sister in Leningrad. We had precious Chrisitan literature hidden under our dresses.*

*I travelled by car, bus, boat and train in Scandinavia, and as here, on a car-free island, by transport motorbike.*

*Changing country means changing number plates. I had to make many sorts of changes through the years.*

*When in Rome ... actually I could eat with chopsticks before going to China, but I became more expert there.*

*My kitchen at the second university in China. It was grey cement and the drain allowed entrance for cockroaches, though not for mice.*

*The English teacher had to help too on practical work days for students and faculty. Here I was learning to carry heavy stones with the help of a shoulder pole.*

*Jack with his proud English 'Mum' when he graduated as MA.*

*When we started the new Chinese Church in Budapest I had to
provide worship leading as well as preaching at first.*

*In Budapest one way I tried to reach the Chinese was by giving English lessons in my home.*

*With Vivien in Prague, where she served the Chinese church as evangelist and pastor for two years.*

# 10

## SCANDINAVIA

### Sweden

From Finland I was already beginning to travel to Sweden, Norway and Denmark for meetings. On my first visit to Sweden I stayed with contacts, who took me to the meeting in the next town, 40km away. I had carefully checked and written down the Swedish words I needed to say what was on my heart, but on arriving at the church I found the notes had been left in my grammar book, not in my Bible as I had thought. I had to struggle through, fortunately writing them down once had helped me to memorize them, and I managed without disgracing myself. That gave me confidence and meant I could do without those sort of notes in the future too. ECM leaders decided that I should move to Sweden to be more centrally placed for the work. I was said to have the largest "parish" of any ECM workers. So in 1975 I sold the house to a Christian family, returning the money to ECM and taking some of the furniture with me, and moved to Mariestad in Sweden. The move, although strategically wise, brought up a question in my heart. I had felt that the Lord had called me to Finland. I had imagined I would work there for many, many years. It was a country I really loved and felt at home in. If I now moved to Sweden, was I stepping out of God's will? After some thought and prayer I concluded that my call was not only to a country, but first and foremost to follow Jesus. If He was now leading me on to another country then my job was to follow Him there too. Finland had been the first country, but might not be the only one I was to live in. This turned out to be an important conclusion when I think of all the later moves I was to make. I was no longer bound by a country, but only by my Lord's leading.

I was able to find a one-bedroom flat in a rather soulless estate of large blocks. However the town itself, on the banks of the big Lake Vänern, was quite charming. Much smaller than Helsinki, it had a friendly feeling. I soon found my way to the Free Evangelical church as my first choice. However, it was stiff and formal, and no-one spoke to me. I decided to try another church next week, and so went to the Baptist church. That was warmer, and one old lady greeted me. This was better, I would go there again. The next Sunday there was one face in the crowd that was familiar, and it felt so good. She introduced me to the pastor and other people and soon I was "part of the furniture". I wonder if we realize how important a first visit can be, and how greeting a stranger can mean so much. I later got to know some of the people in the other church, but not being bound by a denomination I was happy to fellowship with like-minded Christians of any ilk. Although I remained a member of my home-church in Helsinki I was treated like a member in my new home. At one stage, when I was feeling the strain of so much travelling, I was able to take six months concentrating on office work and also employed part-time by the Baptist church to do some preaching and some visiting work.

There were a lot of new things to learn in Sweden, although it has many similarities with Finland. The language itself, though basically the same as the Swedish I had learnt in Finland, is pronounced further back in the mouth and has different intonation and some different words. If you are invited to coffee in Finland you will collect your coffee and cake from a buffet table and sit around the room. But in Sweden everyone must fit round the table. Move over to Norway, and you find further changes. Instead of stirring a lump or two of sugar into your coffee you pop a lump of sugar into your mouth and drink the coffee through it, so you don't need spoons. I didn't like drinking that way, and always had a problem asking for a spoon, until I left sugar out altogether, which made life in Norway much easier. In Finland and Sweden the hostess will not refill the cups until everyone has emptied their cup. In Norway the hostess is continually topping up your cup and apologizes if she finds it already empty. This was a problem when I still took sugar - how much more do I need? - but not afterwards, other than that you can drink too much caffeine that way.

At the beginning of my time in Sweden I didn't even have a car, having passed it on to a technically-minded young brother, fresh from Bible college, who could tackle any possible problems. I had a "sell by"-mileage that I observed with my cars, as I couldn't risk being stranded on some lonely road en route to a meeting. That particular car had served me well and given me no problems. Soon after I passed it on the motor breathed its last! The young man and his father put a new one in and it ran for many more miles. So for some time, not having the money to buy my next second-hand car, I was reliant on buses, trains and ferries, and had to carry heavy cases with brochures, projector and slides. A bicycle and two good legs were enough to get me around locally.

My flat actually had a second bedroom with its own toilet and front door. This was designed for teenage children needing some independence. The joining door was locked when I took the flat, so I only paid for what I used. A Finnish girl came to work with a church ministering to the large Finnish population in the town, and she came to live with me, using the extra room. This worked well, but when she eventually moved away I was not allowed to return to paying for the smaller area. The whole rent was too much for me, and I didn't need the extra room for myself, so in April 1977 I gave up the flat. In the Lord's timing a couple from church were getting married and didn't have much furniture. They were very happy to borrow my furniture, whilst I set off on extensive travel in Scandinavia and Britain. Ever met a homeless missionary? I had no home (but heaven!!) for seven months, and only the key to my case. For the few weeks I touched base in Mariestad during those months I stayed with my furniture and the friends who were using it, so I could use my own desk during the daytime whilst they were out at work. Eventually I found a suitably priced flat in a smaller house with more character, and there I even had a tiny patch of garden to use for growing vegetables. The owners also lived in the house and the arrangement was very satisfactory for the rest of my time in that country.

From this new central position in Sweden I could more easily reach Norway and Denmark, even the Faeroe Islands, as well as Finland and Sweden. Language-wise Swedish was a great asset, as one can move fairly smoothly to the other Scandinavian languages.

## Norway

In Norway they understand Swedish quite well, and I just changed some words and changed pronunciation and intonation. I moved through a "Scandinavian" mixture until a critical listener told me I no longer spoke Scandinavian but proper Norwegian. Visiting towns on the west coast I had to contend with the alternative version of Norwegian known as Nynorsk (New Norse), which was somewhat different from the Bokmål (Book language) that was more widely used in the south.

I didn't learn to speak it, but I could understand and field questions from a student audience at a college on the west coast. It was a help to have a Norwegian ECM representative - a young man who had been at Bible college with me - to arrange meetings and take some local responsibility.

On the way to or from Norway I would usually call in at the Nordic Bible College. My first visit there was soon after I had visited a Finnish congregation in Sweden. One of the ladies told me her nephew was at this college, and to say hello from her. I arrived and was politely welcomed by the students. As they had some American teachers at the college they were used to foreigners speaking Swedish, but when I asked for the nephew and gave him his aunt's greeting in Finnish there was great astonishment. He and other Finnish lads gathered round me with great enthusiasm to chat. An English lady speaking Finnish, well now, that was something different! We became friends as I visited several times, and I got to know their families, and still have occasional contact with them today.

## Denmark

Danish was different. The written language looks like Norwegian, but pronunciation is very different and guttural, and other Scandinavians impolitely usually describe it as "a throat illness". I was mostly in the Copenhagen area, and always stayed with a faithful ECM friend, Inger. Every morning and evening we would read a chapter of the New Testament together, phrase by phrase, as I learned the pronunciation and the words that were different from Swedish. Inger attended my meetings and, at my request, made a note of all my mistakes as I spoke my unique and ever-changing form of "Scandinavian". Eventually the time came when she could say I was speaking Danish without mistakes. Not unsurprisingly I had picked up Inger's Copenhagen dialect. When visiting a theological college in Norway I met a Danish girl from Jutland and spoke Danish to her. She was thrilled, but pointed out my Copenhagen dialect. Oh dear, you can't please everybody! Well, a Northern lass like me would also pick out a foreigner speaking English with a London accent. There was some interest and even financial support for ECM's work from Denmark, despite the general spiritual darkness of that country.

## Other travels

From both Finland and Sweden, as well as travelling into Eastern Europe, I made regular trips down to the Continent to visit our missionaries. In this way I could gain first-hand experience and information, take pictures, and get the feeling of the field. Returning north I could share the pictures and impressions to help the Scandinavian churches understand the darkness of the European continent and the need for more workers there. In Austria and France I could chat with the local people, but in Italy, Spain and Portugal I needed interpretation. Some of the Spanish young people couldn't understand that it was possible I didn't speak any Spanish. So I learned a couple of cheery exclamations and they were happy! In Portugal I was asked to bring greetings in two local churches. I decided to do what I had done years before in Finland - I wrote out what I wanted to say in English, had it translated and practised reading it. Again it is a fairly easy language to read (unlike English) and I managed quite well. "Sorry I don't speak Portuguese" I apologized in fluent Portuguese. They didn't believe me - until they came up to chat with me afterwards and found I had been telling the truth.

ECM bi-ennial conferences or Prayer Days were always welcome times of fellowship with other missionaries as I was otherwise rather out on a limb. In the early days we single women were put in dormitories whilst the marrieds were in double rooms. Eventually it was realized that we were not schoolchildren, and singles too were put into twin rooms. When asked who I would like to share a room with  - most asked to be with their best friend - I always asked to be with someone who had joined since the last conference, and whom I didn't know, as sharing a room is a good way to get to know new people. That way I reckoned I knew just about everybody in the Mission.

# 11

## FAROE ISLANDS

The Faroe Islands are a small group of islands in the middle of the North Atlantic, home to far more sheep than people, hence its name, which means Sheep Islands. It is assumed that the islands were peopled by the Vikings sailing west from Norway. Faroese tradition says that the intelligent ones were dropped off on these islands, whilst the stupid ones carried on as far as Iceland. I understand the Icelanders tell the same story the other way round!! In any case their languages are similar, derived from Old Norse. Faroese was not written down until early in the last century, and there was discussion as to whether the spelling should be according to pronunciation or to show its historical connections. The latter way was chosen. It therefore looks like a Scandinavian language, but the pronunciation has to be learned. There are three genders (as in German) compared to only two in Norwegian etc. There are also more cases than in the other languages - though not nearly as many as in Finnish, which of course is a completely unrelated language.

I knew none of this when I first visited the islands in 1978, not even that they had a language of their own. ECM had once sent a representative to take meetings, but he was no longer able to fit it in, and as Nordic ECM worker it was within my field, so I was asked to go. This was not without some problems. The rather dull form of Lutheranism presumably arrived with the Danes, who own the islands (though they have a great deal of autonomy). But the people were evangelized in the early 20th century by a missionary sent out by the Scottish Brethren. Assemblies grew up in every village. Living at the mercy of the sea and weather (British soldiers in the War dubbed it "The Land of Maybe"), the folk are naturally God-fearing, and the Gospel took good root.

But the Brethren don't like women to speak in church. Aware of this I was rather nervous, and had the obligatory hat with me. They have no pastors, but two evangelists acted as leaders for the assemblies on the whole islands. They both spoke good English and usually travelled round with visiting English speakers, acting as interpreters. Danish speakers were understood by adults, as it was used as their second language, taught in schools and used in communication with Denmark. The evangelists were happy I could travel round alone, using Danish to communicate. Before the first meeting I asked Brother Zach what I could say. "Preach but don't teach," he advised. Oh dear, where does the boundary go? With a prayer for guidance I took the meeting as I would have done elsewhere in Scandinavia. Afterwards over tea and coffee - both equally black, you had to sniff them to identify which was which - I asked, "There wasn't too much teaching was there?" "Oh yes," was the reply. "Very good teaching. I was taking notes!" After that I relaxed. There were different attitudes to me as a woman. In some chapels I was asked for missionary information only, and Brother X.. would preach the Word. In some places I could bring the Word, but was asked to speak from the front, not the pulpit. In one chapel they said, "We can see you and hear you better if you go into the pulpit." - the pragmatic approach! In the capital, Thorshavn, I was asked to speak to the Women's meeting, and then to the Youth meeting. I was not allowed to speak in the main assembly. But looking round the youth meeting I saw a good number of older people - yes, men too - who had slipped in to listen!

A small plantation of fir trees in a valley are the only trees on these bare islands, but in all their bareness there is a wild beauty about them. The roads are good, specially improved for a visit from the Queen of Denmark, and many ferries travel between the islands - maybe, weather permitting! And there was one flight a day arriving from Copenhagen - maybe! What a contrast to busy Copenhagen airport! On one trip we had almost landed, but came down through the clouds too close to the short runway and had to turn sharply upwards again to avoid the mountains. It was a very queer feeling. We flew to the nearest mainland, Bergen in Norway. After a meal and a couple of hours' wait we tried again and this time got down, in the evening instead of the afternoon. But no one was concerned. In the Land of Maybe this was normal. After all, the previous day the plane hadn't been able to land at all!

I was fascinated to find the Faroese have their own language, - I hadn't really thought about it before - and since it had been written down they could also have their own Bible. For many years they had only been able to read God's Word in Danish or Norwegian. Before the Second World War Viktor Danielsen had translated the Bible for the first time into Faroese, but because of the War it had not been printed. After the War it needed revising, and was only printed much later - the NT in 1967 and the whole Bible in 1975. In 1978, on my first visit to the islands, I stayed with the daughter of Viktor Danielsen, and asked her and her son to read some Bible passages onto tape for me. Another family, seeing my interest, presented me with a Faroese Bible as I left, and I also took a Christian magazine home with me. Then began an interesting time of language analysis. I had no teaching on how to do this and no grammar book to help, so I just had to use my initiative, comparing Bible passages, guessing at the more everyday language of the magazine, recognizing words that were related to other Scandinavian languages, getting the hang of things, and listening to the tapes. I was also able to pick up Faroese broadcasts from Monte Carlo, which helped to understand the spoken language.

By the time I went on my next visit I had some idea of the language, but still took the first meetings in Danish. At one village the congregation was mostly young people. Would they understand Danish? Maybe half, I was told. Well, if I try with Faroese maybe they will still understand half. So I launched into my talk in a new language, and was told they had understood. Next evening I was back in Danish, but the following evening, having read my text in Faroese I didn't change back, and just continued, gaining confidence as I went. The way to a man's heart may be through his stomach, but the way to anybody's heart is through their language. I have found this many times, and the Faroese also appreciated someone making the effort to learn their language. No other visiting speaker had ever done this. On the way to the last meeting Evangelist Paul asked me if I was going to speak in English or Danish. Neither, I said, I am going to use Faroese. He looked amazed, so I added that people in Eidi and another church had understood me. He wasn't convinced, but said no more until after the meeting, when he said, "I thought they must have been polite to say that in Eidi, but I understood you too!!!" What a pity, he said, as he drove me to the airport, that I had to leave when I was just getting wind under my wings with the language. Indeed.

On my last visit, in 1981, I took all meetings in Faroese, having stayed for a couple of days first with a family where I could accustom my mind to the language again. But although there was a warm reception and sympathetic hearing, the traditionalists eventually gained the upper hand and I received a sad letter. If ECM could send a man to speak they would welcome him, but I as a woman would not be allowed to speak again. I understood their position, but found it a pity that my God-given ability to share His Word and His message in their language without interpretation should be subjected to their traditions. Unfortunately ECM was not able to send a man, so the contact with the Faroes was lost. I still have the Bible, the magazine and another book to remind me of the dear brothers and sisters there.

# 12

## GREECE

During my time in Sweden I made a long trip by car down to Greece. After the ECM bi-ennial conference in the south of Germany I was to stay with our Greek co-worker and get to know her work. Sophia lived in Milotopos, a small village not too far from Katarini. We met up at the conference in Germany and drove through Yugoslavia together. I was glad of the company on such a long drive through unfamiliar countries, and it also meant it was easy to find her village and her little two-bedroomed bungalow. The houses stretched along the dusty streets and life was lived more outside than inside them. I had studied some NT Greek at Bible college and refreshed it at an evening course in Sweden, but this was modern Greek, and the knowledge of the New Testament version was both a help and a hindrance. At least I could read the letters and knew some grammar. Outside the bread shop one could read the word "artos", which I knew from the Bible. But going in one asked for "psomi" which is the modern word for bread. I began to understand some from Sophia's conversations with others, and enjoyed the Greek cooking and the relaxed style of life. The Greek Evangelical Church, much in the minority, is still rather a stiff kind of Christianity. But it was the best way for a missionary to work there.

I had only been there a couple of days when I was shaken awake about 7am. I didn't at first know what had woken me, but got up and met Sophia in the hallway. "What's up?" I asked. "Seismos!" she answered. An earthquake! We went out to find some people on the streets looking worried, but soon we went back in to make breakfast. As we sat eating and chatting the room began to shake and the cups jangled on their hooks. Sophia leapt up, grabbed me by the arm and we rushed out. Now there were more people outside, and we stayed out quite a long time. Being in a bungalow we eventually ventured back in and there were no more big quakes - these both had been over 4 on the Richter scale and had caused some damage to a few homes in the village, which turned out to have been the epicentre of the quake. At last, this little village of Milotopos was on the map, even shown on Greek TV that evening! The TV men came round and filmed the damaged houses - cracks in some walls. For days afterwards we were super-aware of every little shake. There were some small tremors, but even a heavy lorry trundling by could cause us to look anxious and murmur "Seismos?" For several nights we slept in the big porch, so we would be nearer the door if another quake came, but eventually returned to our beds.

We made a day trip to Philippi and Neapolis, seeing the ruins of the Roman barracks, and a prison room cut into the rock, which could have been the one where Paul and Silas were kept until the Lord sent an earthquake to release them - well, we knew what an earthquake could do in that area! I took out my Bible and we read together the whole story of the happenings in that place. Sophia and her friend were impressed. "We've been here lots of times" they said, "but never read the Bible here. It makes it come alive, doesn't it?" Later we also went down south to visit Athens. Standing on Mars Hill I again took out my Bible and we read together what Paul had said in that same place. It was on that trip that we had a road accident. I stood behind another car at traffic lights. We were looking directly into the sun. An Austrian lorry, thinking he was overtaking us, suddenly spotted the red light against the sun and braked, his trailer skidding and hitting the back side of my car. We were three in the car, and the place he hit was the empty seat. As he was Austrian I could communicate with the driver, even comfort him, as he was rather distraught at his mistake. At a local garage the side was knocked back into some sort of shape, and the exhaust repaired, which was the main damage. It wasn't a good job and had to be re-done once in Greece and finally when back in Sweden, but it was all paid for by the Austrian insurance.

Continuing on, we stood on the bridge over the Corinth canal and watched a big ship far below creeping carefully along through this long and very narrow channel. In Corinth we saw the ruins of the old city from Paul's time. In the museum there was one room that was only opened for groups who had booked in advance. Such a group was just going in as we were there, and we were allowed to join them. The contents of the room were clay replicas of breasts and penises, which had been offered to the gods in the hope of a cure for the offerer. This clearly backed up what Paul said about Corinth and its reputation as an immoral city - venereal diseases, it seems, were rife.

For several weeks I accompanied Sophia as she took Vacation Bible School in villages around the area. Up to 15 children would gather in one of the homes for a daily session of fun and teaching. We even went to one village close to the Albanian border. Some of the people there had relatives in Albania whom they had had no contact with since the border was suddenly closed without warning many years earlier. We heard of one woman who had gone to visit a relative amongst the Greek population of southern Albania and been unable to return home. The family just had to manage without her. And in 1980, when I was there, there was no sign of any change in the situation. Eating in different homes each day, every generous hostess put on a feast, until I was almost ill and couldn't eat anything.

After about a month we drove down to Leptokaria, on the coast below Katarini. It was the summer camp area of the Greek Evangelical Church. There were two blocks of apartments for those who could afford them, the rest of us lived in tents. Sophia was summoned to her sick mother's side in America and had to leave me alone, waiting for an ECM team to arrive to do some evangelism amongst Kosova-Albanians holidaying in the area. Meanwhile I had people from our village of Milotopos also staying there, and I made friends with a few other people. Every morning there was a devotional time together under a large canopy. This wasn't compulsory, but many attended. I was asked to give a testimony. Having written it with some help, I read it out one morning - in Greek, of course. After the meeting most people went into the sea before lunch and siesta. Lying in a tent in the boiling heat, even with both ends open, was not conducive to sleep, as it was too hot. We did have thunderstorms though. The water even worked its way through the canvas of my tent roof and dripped in. At least we had camp beds and didn't sleep on the ground. The next night the husband of the family I was friendly with came over and insisted I move to their tent, which was covered with plastic and guaranteed dry. The children shared a bed and I had one of theirs, until my tent had dried out.

When that family went home after two weeks I had to look round and make new friends - one lady spoke English, but all other communication had to be in Greek. I was expecting the ECM team any day, but they didn't turn up for another two weeks due to a breakdown and having to return to Vienna. So I had what turned out to be a lazy and interesting holiday with lots of swimming, kilos of peaches and melons, and new friends helping me with their language. Risky business can turn out to have unexpected easy sides!

Eventually I returned to Milotopos to pack up and drive north again. At the border to Yugoslavia there was a queue a mile long. Rather than run their motors all the time the people had got out and were pushing their cars a few yards at a time. I tried to do the same, but it was hard work on my own, even with a fairly small car. A friendly family saw my efforts and sent their son aged about 10 to help me. They were Yugoslavs and I couldn't chat with him. How could I get the Gospel over? I remembered that I had some tracts in the car, in Serbian and Croatian (the languages sound similar but are written in different scripts), so I got them out. I also remembered a little chorus in Croatian that I had learned some years ago from a 5-year old lad in Vienna. "He has saved my soul, my Jesus, I know he loves me." I sang it to the boy as we pushed, and then, using the words of the song asked if he knew that Jesus loved him. He pointed upwards, showing it was to do with God. When we had got right up to the crossing point and he was about to return to his family I showed him the two tracts, one in Latin script, one in cyrillic and asked which he could understand. He took one, I've forgotten which, and happily ran off. Praise God, with a few inadequate words from a song I could share something of God's love with those who had shown kindness to me.

It was late when I crossed the border, and with a two-hour difference in time (not sure why it was two hours) I couldn't make it to the missionary home I was aiming for and had to stop at a motel. I felt very alone and vulnerable in this new country in the dark, but Jesus was with me. Early next morning I continued on my way and arrived for breakfast with ECM Yugoslav friends. The wife of the family wanted to travel to Belgrade, so was welcome to come as my passenger. She was a lovely lady, but spoke no English. How I wished she could speak Greek, then I could at least have had some sort of conversation. My little Croatian song of the day before didn't get us very far, though we did sing it together. So for several hours we drove almost in silence, just pointing out to each other the beauty we saw on the way. I felt so helpless, and I suppose she did too. In Belgrade I took her to a sister who spoke English, and stayed there myself overnight. Then another long drive to Lienz in Austria, this time on my own, and next day on to Germany, where I stayed a couple of days before making the long drive back up to Sweden, completing 11.000 km of driving in about 10 weeks. It had been a very interesting two and a half months, including an earthquake, history lessons in Philippi, Athens and Corinth, language lessons at the camp, and lots of other experiences in the Lord's work. And of course I had plenty to share with the Scandinavian churches the next autumn.

# 13

## GERMANY

God's ways of leading me on have been many and various. After 11 years of travelling round Scandinavia for ECM - not forgetting the visits to the Continent to get first-hand information on our missionaries, and the trips into Eastern Europe, - I was ready for a change, though I didn't know what. Non-stop travelling was taking its toll, I had been travelling and working mostly on my own, and I had not seen the fruit I longed for - missionaries going to Europe through ECM. Because of this last point I felt a failure. It was not until some years later that I began to recognize that the Lord had been using me in many ways even though I didn't achieve the goal I had set myself. God's goal had been different, and only He knows how much had been achieved. Even though it sounded spiritual I was looking for "success" in my work instead of godly success in my own life. I wasn't actively looking for a change, but the Lord saw that I needed one. Because of being out on a limb on my own I was usually invited down to some regional ECM meeting each year to give me fellowship with other missionaries. Just before I travelled down to Prayer Days in Austria in January1980 the word "administration" dropped into my mind "out of the blue". I had no idea what it meant for me and tried to put it out of my mind. When I arrived at the Prayer Days the Director, Rev. Jack Murray, gave a brief welcoming talk. He told about the European Office which was now located in Kandern, a small town in the Black Forest. When he added the comment "I need someone to help with administrative work," my knees felt weak. After the talk he came over to me and said, "I was thinking of you. Will you move down to Kandern?" I would probably have been very uncertain if the Lord had not prepared me with that one little word in advance. He is so good!

It was hard leaving the Nordic countries after 18 years, 11 of them in ECM ministry, but as with leaving Finland, it was a step forwards following Jesus. I knew the German language and something of the culture, so it wouldn't be completely new.

So, having arranged for my furniture to come after me as soon as I found a flat, I packed what I could into my little car and took the boat across the Baltic Sea to Kiel in North Germany. Arriving early in the morning on 2nd February 1981 I drove with few stops down the excellent German Autobahns and arrived in Kandern (very near Basel) in time for dinner - over 900km. At first I stayed with two American ladies for a month, then found a furnished room nearby, which gave me my own space until I found a flat on the upper floor of a private house, the landlords living on the ground floor. Now I could get my furniture and settle in for the next ...?... years. It turned out to be only 18 months, as the landlord and his wife were divorcing and she wanted to live upstairs, so I was thrown out. (Neighbours said this rather strange couple found any excuse to throw tenants out and keep the advance rent. I, they said, had stayed longer than most!) I don't know what happened, whether the wife did move upstairs, or whether they took a new tenant and more advance rent to keep. When I met the wife in town a few times and greeted her cheerfully she turned away, as if she had a bad conscience. I was able to find another flat further away from the office, which I was to share with another girl due to arrive in Kandern soon. She never came. The new landlords were sweet, but soon came with tears in their eyes to say they had to sell the whole house, so had to give me notice. I didn't find anything else, and they couldn't sell the house, so I stayed there for another 15 months on a knife edge, paying half the rent because I was using only half the flat, not knowing when I might have to leave at short notice, so not getting round to make the place cosy and personal. It wasn't easy, but then I had lived in a suitcase before!

Right at the beginning of my time in Kandern I heard there was a new Free Evangelical church in Lörrach, the bigger town on the Swiss border, about ten miles down the road from Kandern, and I went there. By the time I had my own flat I had got to know some of the folk, and invited them to a house-warming coffee and cake. The coffee was poured, the big gateau stood in the middle of the table. "Help yourselves" I said, and waited for them to do just that. They sat and looked at each other and at me. "Bitte schön" I said again. Then one brave young man picked up the cake spade and started putting a piece of gateau on each guest's plate. Oops! That was a bit of German culture I didn't know - the hostess is supposed to put at least the first piece of cake onto the guests' plates to show she really wants them to have it. In Scandinavia people would react to such treatment with "Am I a child that I can't help myself?" Oh the perils of living in different cultures!

It was good to be part of a team for a change, saying hello to the others when I arrived at the office each morning, going out for an occasional meal together. I worked on various literature projects, producing leaflets and slide presentations. And Jack Murray would ask my opinion on, or my reaction to his ideas - he called it "bouncing them off me" - before putting them into practice. It was an interesting three years, more restful and stable than the travelling life I had been living, and I am grateful for the experience. There were a lot of missionaries in the area, mainly American and Canadian, because there was a school for missionaries' children in Kandern run by the Janz Team. Many of the parents travelled but a number were involved in the school. They had their own Fellowship on Sundays, to which I would have been welcome. But the culture shock I experienced there was not so much with the German culture as the North American one, with which I was not at all familiar. So I preferred to go to the German church and outside office hours spend my time with people of the country I was living in. I think the North Americans, who were not as integrated as I was as a single person with good fluency in the language, regarded me as "stand-offish" for this reason, though I got on well with those I met. Later the pastor of the German church invited me to share some visiting work, so I would visit ladies, counsel and do Bible study with several individuals, where it was more appropriate for a woman to visit than a man. Through this church I got to know the whole denomination as it is in Germany - it was interesting to note the similarities and differences compared to the equivalent churches in Finland and Sweden.

Through these connections I heard of a small church right up in Aurich in the north-west corner of Germany, where a large number of people had come to faith in Jesus as a result of a summer tent campaign. From a membership of five, attendance about 10, they now suddenly had 40 new regulars, all thirsty to know more about Jesus. They needed someone to help. The call touched my heart, and I made further enquiries. They were about to get their own pastor, a young man straight from theological college, but would be glad of my help too, as a missionary, of course, not expecting to be paid by the fledgling church. After three years in the office I as a "people person" needed to get back to more independent functioning in a church, and this seemed to be the right move. People couldn't understand how I could move from such a beautiful mountainous area as the Black Forest to the flatness of

Ostfriesland, but then I have never asked for beautiful surroundings (though I have certainly had some) but to do the Lord's work. And Ostfriesland with its wide, wide sky has its own charm in a different way, and its own culture. In fact there are lots of jokes told in Germany about the Ostfresians, a bit like Irish jokes in Britain. And whereas most Germans have a coffee culture the Ostfriesians drink tea. No, not like the English. You put a lump of translucent rock sugar - called a kluntje - into a tiny cup and pour strong tea over it so that it crackles. Then you carefully slide a spoonful of cream into the tea. Don't stir, just drink, and then pour more tea over the same kluntje. Only after three cups (equal to barely one English mugful) can you put your spoon over the top of your cup to show you don't want more. If you don't the hostess will keep on pouring. Not being an avid tea drinker - especially not strong Assam tea - I tried to get away with only two cups. At church, where no one noticed, this was easy, but at an old lady's house once it didn't work. I put my spoon over the cup after two rounds. "You've only had two cups," she said reproachfully, and I had to submit to a third!

The church in Aurich had moved out of its small meeting room to a larger house, the ground floor being renovated to make a meeting room and kitchen. The cellar became the youth area, the first floor was made into a flat for the pastor and his wife, and the attic was turned into a flat for me. However, it took time to do, and again I was homeless for a few weeks. I went back to Lörrach to share with folk there about the new situation, and stayed until I got news that my flat was just about ready. It was lovingly done by the members and I was very happy with it. The Ostfriesian dialect was very different from that of the Black Forest, which is near to Swiss German. This new dialect fitted my mouth more easily, and in no time I had adopted it to some extent. I later attended a course for the Low German language spoken widely in the area. It is very close to Dutch, and though I learned to understand it I never really spoke it, but love even today to hear the sound of it.

The newly ordained pastor and his wife moved in soon after I did. I had a weekly time of discussion and prayer with the pastor, and despite his being half my age we got on very well. His wife was a cheery, enthusiastic young lady, yet very different from me. She and I had to work through a few situations where we had more than a slight disagreement. There was sometimes hurt on one or both sides, but being Christians of some maturity we were able to talk it over, cry together and forgive each other. I think this brought us closer together than if we had always politely seen eye-to-eye. Disagreements, even hurts, are not always bad, but they do need to be dealt with, as otherwise they can grow into bigger troubles and bitterness.

Apart from the pastor there were the few mature Christians who had been in the church before the influx of new believers. The older couple were a delight, and became my good friends. With a lot of young people coming in they appreciated me as a middle-aged person who could understand them and their worries and concerns better. And equally, for me they were a source of support and fellowship, not to mention fun. We used to say that we "mis-understood" each other very well right from the beginning. Today, twenty years on, though "old and crumbling" they still insist on having me stay with them when I visit.

Although a woman preaching was not acceptable in Germany, the pastor encouraged me to share with him in the leading of a house group in a village some miles away. It was also acceptable for me to share briefly in the Sunday service, and I began to take a slot on mission, highlighting different countries each month. I helped produce the church newsletter, which would also include something on mission. Apart from this I concentrated on counselling and teaching individuals, either in my home or theirs, sometimes on a regular basis, sometimes just as needed. One girl used to come to breakfast once a week to talk and pray with me before going to work. With so many new Christians there were plenty of problems, and also joy as we saw them growing. One young couple, living together but not married, both came to faith. They soon recognized that this was not the right way for Christians to live, and asked to be married in the church. The girl was already five months pregnant. Their non-Christian relatives were very impressed with the wedding and reception in our limited space. That we could have such fun at the reception without either alcohol or dancing was something they had never experienced before! At the reception the bridegroom stood up and gave a moving testimony about their former life and their new life, and explained that this was the reason for the wedding.

After three years I felt the Lord was again "loosening the soil around my roots". I would put roots down when I arrived in a new place, and at some point I would feel this job is done, it is time to move on - what I called God loosening my roots ready for the next marching orders.

I began to think about using English teaching again, as I was not happy being regarded as a "professional" Christian, speaking about Jesus because I was paid to do so. My thoughts turned to Finland and I applied to a Finnish-British Society as before. This was in an ideally situated place that would enable me to visit churches around the country between teaching terms. Although they encouraged me to send in my application immediately  they then told me they had appointed someone else even before they got my papers. The door slammed shut and it hurt. Around the same time a missionary newsletter included a notice about teachers needed for China. I pushed it to one side, no, I wasn't thinking of China. I don't know why I didn't put it straight in the bin, but it stayed around and I kept finding it. Eventually I decided it wouldn't hurt to ask more. In the meantime I started praying. Not the "anywhere You say. Lord" sort of prayer, but "You don't really mean I should go to China, do You Lord?" I certainly didn't want to leave Europe and had no romantic notions about China. But I was asking honestly.

# SECTION FIVE
## China and the Chinese

# 14

## THE FIRST YEAR IN CHINA

It was Saturday evening and I was reclining in the bathtub in my rather romantic bathroom under the sloping roof in Aurich when God's answer hit me. Listening to Trans World Radio I happened across the English programme telling the life of C.T.Studd. I had read his life story but forgotten the details, so the first programme about his conversion tempted me to tune in the following week too. This was now about his missionary call to China. He asked the Lord for a word whilst waiting for a train. Opening his Bible at random he found a verse which confirmed God's will to him. I don't remember the verse, but I do remember the next words, which said that as the train set off, its wheels seemed to say: "It's China! it's China! it's China!" I sat up in the bath. That was God's voice coming out of the radio!! "Okay Lord," I answered, "I give in, I'll go!" And that was that. The church in Aurich was somewhat shocked. I'd given regular mission focus talks, but the day I did China, although they nodded as I pointed out the need, they nearly fell off their chairs when I said I was actually going! I was accepted by the organisation I applied to, but they had no placing for me, so I said I would be prepared to do language study first, unless the Lord opened an unexpected door straight to a teaching post. It was whilst I was on a TEFL course in Hastings that I got a phone call to say they had a new contact, a university which had asked for a lady in her 40's and I was the only one fitting that description on their books. God is so good - He knew what it was going to be like and so assured me that He had chosen just that place for me. I needed that comfort later.

The TEFL course (Teaching English as a Foreign Language) was difficult, as I was feeling rather insecure. Not only had I left Germany and my years of work in Europe, and the mission I had been with for 18 years, and was heading for the completely unknown, but southern England was also like a foreign country to me. Actually the whole of Britain was foreign to me at that time, but the North would at least have been a bit more familiar. Also we were trained to teach multi-lingual small groups, using a low teacher profile, whereas the one thing I knew about my future job was that the classes would be large and need a high teacher profile. However, the certificate had to be gained, so I pushed on with it, finding living in digs difficult but enjoying warm fellowship at a local Baptist Church that I "happened" to find the first Sunday.

My ECM colleagues waved me off at Gatwick airport on 25th August 1987. And so I flew off into a new life thousands of miles from my beloved Europe. On the application form for the sending organisation one question had been "What do you expect to get out of this time for yourself?" The question surprised me, and my answer surprised the leaders. Many people saw it as fulfilling a dream, or as credit for their career. I said that I hadn't thought of getting anything for myself, I was simply going in obedience to God. And so it was. I wonder why we are expected to look for self-fulfillment or self-betterment in the things we do for God. Can we not do them just because He tells us to? If He died out of love for us without thinking of His own benefit or advantage, shouldn't we also obey simply out of love for Him?

The balmy night air surrounded me as the sampan chugged across the water to an outlying Hong Kong island, where I stayed for a few days of orientation. All the other teachers were half my age, but that didn't prevent us getting on well and supporting each other. Then I was accompanied to my new position by one of the staff members from base. After waiting at the airport for people to meet us, who never turned up, we had to get a taxi (a motorized rickshaw) to take us the 12 miles of bumpy road out to my university. When I looked at the flat I was to occupy I turned to my colleague and said, "I want to go home. I can't live here." It turned out the room wasn't ready, so I was put up in a hotel in the big town twelve miles away for a week, which gave me an opportunity to familiarize myself with it. When I moved into my flat it looked rather better than at first, and I was beginning to get used to the surroundings. Now I had lino on the stone-flagged floor and a thin mattress of padded cotton on the previously bare boards of the bed, and I was grateful for the mosquito netting draped over a frame, which made the bed look like a fairy-tale four-poster! The large bathroom, built under the outside stairs to the upper floor, where students lived, had a bath but no hot water, a western toilet (sit-down type) but no water pressure to flush it. Fortunately it also had a shiny enamel urinal (why had they asked for a woman?!) which proved very useful. Firstly I could deflect its water supply to enable me to fill a bucket to flush the toilet, and secondly, when the electricity was off (which was often) I could set a candle in there, which was well reflected and gave a good light! Ever heard of Romans 8:28? Yes, everything works together for good...

The kitchen had a cement sink and cold-water tap, and an electric wok and kettle. I bought most of my food in town, catching the university minibus or the ordinary bus, to which I had a 15min walk through paddy fields, but fruit and vegetables I often bought from local peasants who came and sat with their wares by the roadside on campus. With no functioning fridge food could not be kept long. With a very dodgy electricity supply my diet that winter was not of the best.

Life around me was enough to turn any westerner's stomach. The students washed at the taps providing dirty water in the yard. Teeth cleaning was done outside their rooms very noisily. Spitting, after noisy throat-clearing, was common, and even in the classroom I saw them spitting on the cement floor and rubbing it in with their shoes. Whilst they think the habit of blowing one's nose and putting the hanky back in the pocket is bad, I found their nose-blowing onto the ground without a hanky was even worse. They would collect food from the canteen in an enamel bowl and eat noisily with a spoon. Some told me they almost forgot how to use chopsticks by the time they went home. The remains of their food, anything they didn't want (and it really wasn't appetizing, I tried it) was thrown over the balcony onto a concrete sloping surface. One had to be careful to keep under the balcony when walking that way, as a cascade of food or water could come over anytime. During that first year I only saw the desperately poor side of Chinese life, and nothing of the rapidly modernizing big eastern cities.

Apart from one old man I was the only teacher living on site, the others wisely choosing to be shipped in by minibus each day from other colleges where the accommodation and sanitation were better. Conditions were really terrible and even the students complained as through the winter things got worse. Eventually, when they commented on the fact that I could still smile, even though I came from the West, I could tell them that my smile didn't depend on outward circumstances but on inward peace with God. Of course I couldn't start off by telling them about Jesus, I just had to live His life amongst them, and they noticed it. My door was always open for them to come and talk, and they appreciated my style of teaching too.

One day a Down's syndrome child came onto the campus (local peasants used to collect scraps of food thrown out by the students, cut grass for their animals etc.) She must have wandered away from her motheer and came to our teaching building. I found some students screaming at her and trying to push her away with a broom like a rat, whilst she clung frightened to the wall. As I approached they melted away. I was quite upset at this but they were not my students and I had not yet learnt much Chinese. I then took several lessons for my students on the subject of handicapped people. They listened in amazement and giggled with embarrassment as I explained that, whether handicapped from birth or through an illness or accident, these people are still people, and they have feelings, need friends, and need love. They began to ask "Who is this lady who cares about us and who cares about the sort of people who are hidden and despised in our country?" This was much better than me preaching to them in words, and when Christmas approached and we talked about "the reason for the season" they were able to see the reason behind my behaviour. This was more effective and a number of them came to know the Lord during that time.

Meanwhile I got a rash on my back caused by the dirty water I was using - from a tank above my kitchen. It was duly emptied, scrubbed out, and refilled with water imported by truck from the nearest town 5km away - did I explain that we were in the midst of paddy fields? Seeing the efforts they made to bring me reasonably clean water, carrying it in buckets up the steps from the truck to the container on my roof, I had to be very economical with it, so they didn't have to refill it too often. The student who spoke best English had been assigned to help me, and she applied lotion to the rash, which duly cleared up. But soon after this I developed shingles - the waistline version. This wasn't surprising as I had been under considerable stress for about six months with all the farewells, training and adapting to new everything, and not eating very well. The campus doctor looked after me as best she could, but I was off work for a couple of weeks in December. I tried to start again, but found myself weeping after the first lesson, so was given two more weeks sick leave. What I had not stopped was rehearsals for the Christmas nativity play. The sort of presentation Sunday School kids do in Britain I was doing with university students in China, though with more grown-up text. They loved it, learned their lines in English and were all ready for the presentation on Christmas Eve (no holiday in China). We were to do it in a large barn-like building, but didn't get electricity until half-an-hour after we should have started, and then the microphones didn't work. Despite all, a good time was had by all - or so it seemed. There was backlash from the university later.

On Christmas Eve a message came via a teacher from the town, that I was to phone the office in Hong Kong. We had no telephone at the university (I lie not!!) so I took the minibus into town and put through a call from a hotel, supposing they had heard of my shingles and wanted to tell me to rest. I had already decided to go to Hong Kong for the second two weeks' sick leave and told them this. They agreed, but said the real reason for wanting me to phone was to tell me that my mother was dying, not expected to last over Christmas. Letters my sisters had sent to Hong Kong were not forwarded by post for security reasons, and no one had brought them in by hand. I immediately put through another call to my almost 87-year old mother's home, where my sisters were looking after her. She was weak but could speak to me. Meanwhile friends had gone to buy a plane ticket for me to travel next day, so my first Christmas day was spent travelling by plane and train to Hong Kong. As I left the university by minibus I was very moved to have the shepherds, wise men, angels, and Mary and Joseph of the previous evening standing round wishing me a good trip and quick recovery - and give our regards to your mother! Arriving at a Christian guesthouse I was made welcome, and there could not only rest and take plenty of vitamins to build up my strength, but also phone my mother every day until she died on New Year's Eve. I was not in a fit state of health to travel, and anyway, didn't know if I could have reached her in time. I have seen my illness as a gift from God to enable me to be in touch with my mother for that last week of her life - this would have been very difficult or impossible from inside China. She had had a premonition of this before I left, and we waved farewell when I visited her just before my departure, knowing it might be the last time we would meet.

The family I was staying with in Hong Kong had the husband's father visiting them. The very next day he keeled over and died with a heart attack. So we were able to comfort and help each other for the next week. God is not only good, He is amazing!

Going back into China after my break was different from the first time, when I had not known what to expect. Now I knew, and it was much harder. I wrote a meditation:

"I'm going in tomorrow, into China, Lord. That means going back to the privations of Chinese life - stone walls, lino floor, a toilet that doesn't flush, water I need to heat if I want it hot and boil before I can drink it. Going back to a very uncertain electricity supply in a flat geared to electricity. Back to the unpleasant sounds and smells that one just cannot get away from there. Back to the unpredictability, the bureaucracy, the inefficiency that in so many ways is China. Oh Lord, must I? I'm going to need you.

I'm going in tomorrow, into China, Lord. That means going back to the people I have come to appreciate and like for their beautiful features, their ready laughs, their friendliness and willingness to do so much for me. Going back to the students I have grown to love; to those who have shown such an openness to the Gospel and the story of the birth of Jesus. Going back to those who have already accepted Him as their Saviour and need discipling, and to those who are still asking questions, wanting to know more about this Person they see in my life. Oh Lord, thank You - I'm looking forward to that, and I know I can reckon with Your help in every situation. Thank You, Lord!"

Although I was isolated in that situation I managed well, as a pioneer soul. But still it was helpful to have colleagues in the big city 12 miles away, and we met for fellowship almost every weekend, at first just three of us, then joined by three more. I have happy memories of fellowship with these young teachers, whether cooking English food or sharing in Bible study and prayer. Readers probably are aware that the Chinese have difficulty in pronouncing our "r" and often replace it with an "l". You know - "flied lice", "flying tonight" etc. Well, they are aware of this and try to remember to say "r" when they want to say "l". So sometimes they go over the other way. One girl told me she was going to have fun with her friends - chill out - but they use the word "play". She told me she was going to "pray" with her friends, and being absolutely honest but totally misunderstood I replied, "Yes, I do that too sometimes!" A foreigner's problem with the Chinese language is more in the tones, as getting the wrong tone can make the word mean something quite different.

During the spring term our director visited all the teachers. He asked me if I knew of anyone to take up a new post in southern China. I didn't - until an hour later, when he had been told by the university leaders that they couldn't keep me on next year. The tone was polite and the excuse transparent, as they obviously didn't want the Christian influence. The teacher they got to replace me was a disappointment to all, and the authorities realized that after all, Christian ethics are what they want, but without the reason behind the ethics. But for me this other placement had already opened up and I went along for an interview, accompanied by a Chinese teacher. This was one of the things I found difficult to get used to - always being accompanied by someone. I thought it was for security reasons, which to some extent it was, but I later found that the Chinese themselves don't like to go out alone, so it was also part of the culture. On the return journey in an air-conditioned bus the morning was just getting hot when the side window of the bus fell out. It took some time to get the driver to stop, then he and some other men walked back to collect the window. We waited and waited, and they eventually returned without the window. It seems a local man had spotted it and decided it would be good in his garden - no way was he giving it back!! With no policeman nearby to enforce ownership we had to do the remaining 10 hours of the journey through the heat of the day with an open window instead of air-conditioning. Not a journey I would like to repeat! Where else could something like this happen??

Long bus journeys in China deserve a chapter of their own. The buses were mostly old boneshakers, though some more modern ones were being introduced. Seats were often hard, and everything was piled in the aisle - live chickens, sacks of rice or vegetables, cases, and more. On bumpy and winding roads some couldn't take it and were sick. The driver didn't stop so they were sick on the bus steps. This was the place also to take the baby for a "wee-wee" as nappies were not used and the babies were just held out under a tree, by a roadside - or on the bus steps, with encouraging ssssss noises being made to help it happen! We did stop for food and/or the toilet on long trips, usually in a small village. The public toilets were indescribable - a trench divided by waist-high walls and surrounded by a higher wall. The stench made you hold your breath and hurry in and out. For me these stops were even more distasteful as the villagers had never seen a foreigner, so crowded round to stare unashamedly at me if I got off the bus, or peer through the windows if I stayed on. I became almost paranoid over this as time went on. I could usually manage the food, as Chinese food is fried over a hot flame and thus reasonably hygienic.

Back at my university, the rest of the term went reasonably well despite the privations. A number of students and one teacher came to the Lord. The teacher came up to me at a party and asked what religion I was. When I said I was a Christian he was very happy, as he had a lot of questions about the Bible he had been given by another foreigner he had met. He came to my room for teaching and was the very first to ask Jesus into his heart. Although he thought it all right for him to be a Christian, he warned me not to talk to the students about Jesus. However, the Lord worked in his heart, and soon he was encouraging me to talk about Jesus, and witnessing himself!

As I mentioned, I had, in modern terminology, first to "walk the walk" before I could "talk the talk". But one day a student asked me to teach them a song out of a book he had. I didn't know that song, but looked through the book to find another possible one. Ah, what's this? "Nobody knows the trouble I've seen; nobody knows but Jesus." - yes, I'll teach you this one. They enjoyed the singing and then I asked if anyone knew who this Jesus was. Nobody did, so I said they could come to my room and ask if they wanted. That evening I was sitting chatting to Vivien, the student who had been assigned to help me in any way I needed. As she had the best English and was a bright and helpful girl she fitted the job well. I had wanted to talk to her about any faith she may have, but we never got near the subject and I couldn't be direct. Two other students came in to talk. One had been in the above-mentioned class and suddenly said, "Teacher, tell us who Jesus is." I told the others about the song, and then gave the gospel from creation to salvation in a few simple words. The boy sniffed - women's stuff! The girl who had asked was impressed and took a gospel to read (she later became a Christian) and they both left. Vivien turned to me and to my great surprise said, "Teacher, I want to ask Jesus into my heart." It turned out she had been given a book of Bible stories as a child, and had sometimes been to church with her mother, but had never heard of the need for a personal response. So there and then we knelt down and she asked Jesus to come into her life. In the weeks that followed I watched the bud opening into a beautiful flower as Jesus' life in her brought out the sweet personality he had given her. She kept a spiritual diary in

English, which she often showed me when she wanted to ask about some matter of faith. In all the squalor of the surroundings, watching this blossom open was one of the loveliest experiences of my life.

Vivien helped me witness to other students, and also took me home to her family in another city. She led her mother from a general faith to a specific understanding and experience of salvation, and witnessed to others in her wider family. When I moved to my next job she would occasionally turn up to visit me, and I again visited her home. It became known that she was now my Chinese "daughter" - a term to indicate close friendship between people of different generations, just as Paul called Timothy his "son". An amusing meeting remains in my memory from one visit to her home, and this always brings a smile to my lips. Walking in the street I often hear "wai guo ren" whispered near me. "Foreign person" they tell each other as I pass. The children learn this and do it too. In self-defence a friend and I started to turn to them and say "Zhongguo ren" (Chinese person), which usually stops them doing it. As I walked with Vivien through the beautiful town of Guilin a little girl of about five piped up with "foreign person". I smiled at her and replied "Chinese person". She shook her head. Aren't you a Chinese person?" I asked. Again a headshake. "Are you a foreign person then?" Another headshake. At last I understood. "Guilin person" I suggested, and was greeting with a vigorous nodding this time. She knew what Guilin was, and even what foreign was, but China was not yet a concept in her little head!

When I eventually left China Vivien was forbidden by the Security Police to keep in touch with me, as I had been a "bad influence" on her! Through two other students I was able to exchange news with her about once a year. I will tell you more about her later.

# 15

## FURTHER YEARS IN CHINA

When I arrived by fast boat direct from Hong Kong at my new destination in August 1988 much of the town was under water. It lay at the confluence of two rivers and the summer rains flooded the town about every five years. We were given a tour of the town by flat-bottomed boat, waving at people sitting on their balconies - you could hop off at a balcony if you wanted. Again I had to stay in a hotel room until my flat was ready. This time the university campus was all newly built, and I was on the third floor, so no mice but still cockroaches. The water was from the mains and clean (you still boil it to drink) and there were no electricity cuts, since we were on the same line as the waterworks, which couldn't be cut off. The flat was sparse, concrete floored, lino added in the bedroom, but clean. The toilet was the more usual Chinese squat toilet - i.e. a hole in the floor, with a tap and bucket nearby to flush it. By my second term they actually installed a water heater so I could have a warm shower. I was amongst teachers and other staff in this block, and learned to get along with them in my limited Chinese, as well as with the students in English. It was altogether better organised and efficient than the first place, and to me it was luxury, though someone coming direct from Europe would hardly have thought so! Here I was the only resident foreigner in the town and had no fellowship apart from an occasional visitor. Knowing I had many prayer partners in different countries gave me strength, and I was aware of the presence of Jesus with me daily, though I did have some times when I felt rather low. Again I started low-key with sharing God's love, but at Christmas the first student accepted Jesus on her own. She gave me a Christmas card, which I opened when I got back to my flat. I don't remember her exact words but they reflected on her part in the nativity play as the angel bringing Good News to Mary. She said I had come like an angel with Good News for her, and now she wanted to come and worship Jesus and put Him in the centre of her life. Once some others had also found Christ we were able to have fellowship together. I would love to share some of the stories about people there, but as I don't know where they are now, or what situation they are in, it would not be wise. When China has full religious freedom I can write about them.

Beijing was a long way away, but the happenings in Tian'anmen Square in June 1989 were not unknown to us. The daily happenings were shown on TV during the negotiations and talks. Students from our university and another college also staged a march through town with banners welcoming "Mr.Democracy". Even some of the teachers walked behind - though they later hurriedly explained they were only there to keep order!! The day things came to a head in Beijing I was in Canton visiting other teachers. We listened to the BBC World Service and heard of the massacre of the students. When I got home next day and told people about it they didn't believe me. But suddenly TV had a news blackout and reported nothing more for four days. When the edited version of the story had been agreed on the TV news came back, showing the "rabble" attacking army vehicles, and officers visiting wounded soldiers in hospital. The students, they said, has dispersed peacefully, but a small minority amongst the rabble had caused trouble. There was no mention of any casualties amongst students. But now people began to believe what I had told them, and some could listen to the BBC themselves. Our students were shocked, and not a little afraid of possible consequences to themselves for having been on the demonstration.

It took some time for repercussions to reach us, but during the autumn things tightened up, for example people entering university campus were more rigorously checked. Having become a little bolder in my presentation of the Gospel it was not surprising that they were watching me too. In China, as in Rome of old, Christians are easily blamed for problems, and Christian students had been ministering to the others on Tian'anmen Square. Several times the university's Party Secretary came with an interpreter to warn me not to talk to my students about Jesus. Even though I stopped making any open mention they still came. "Have you had some complaint?" I asked. "No". "Then why have you come?" "In case you forget," was their pathetic reply. Each time I felt I had been whipped, but I stood my ground and didn't let them intimidate me. On the third or fourth visit I determined to stand in Jesus Name. "Gentlemen," I began, in a polite but firm tone, "I am not ashamed of anything I have done here. If you can show me even one student who has become a worse student or a worse person through my influence, then I will be ashamed." They departed with their tails between their legs and didn't come back!

During my second year at this university I was no longer alone. A lovely white-haired retired teacher, Mary, came to join me for one term. Chinese years are divided into only two terms - September to Spring Festival (late January or early February) and then March to July. Mary had previously worked in Hong

Kong and spoke good Cantonese, a variety of which was spoken by the locals in our area. So she could go shopping more easily than I could, as not all spoke Mandarin. One day a little old lady pointed at her and said "White hair!" and then pulled off her own black woolly hat to reveal also a head of white hair. They both laughed. Mary was a conscientious teacher and enjoyed the work, and we had good fellowship together. When she left she was replaced by a much younger lady with little teaching experience. She found life in China very difficult, lonely and disappointing. Despite my efforts to encourage her she left for home after only four months, to the anger and disappointment of the university. I took her classes and exams to the end of term.

It was perhaps not surprising in the light of my "religious activities" that after two years the highest authority in the province refused me a further year's work permit, although the university itself would have liked me back. I was allowed in as a visitor to collect my belongings, and was then seen off by disappointed students and teachers as I caught the boat down to Hong Kong. I stayed for some months in Hong Kong, helping in the office of the sending agency for our teachers. During these months I visited my old students a few times, but had to be very careful, for their sakes. One time I stayed in a hotel and sent a message for the Christian students to come and bring their own cup, and we would have a party. About eight came, but two had forgotten to bring cups. I went out to ask the hotel staff for two cups, but I got the intonation wrong and asked for two quilts instead. They looked very suspicious - what are you doing in there? The mistake was cleared up and we had a good laugh. I am still not sure which tone means which object.

I also visited a former student who had been very interested in Christianity. He was a remarkably self-assured and even arrogant young man, yet one whom I liked a lot. He had argued and objected to the gospel, but eventually capitulated, admitted he was a sinner, and asked Jesus into his heart. One day he said to me "Teacher, before, I only had one god in my life, that was me. Now I have two gods in my heart, Jesus and me." I suggested it would be even better if he pushed the "me" bit out altogether and he agreed, but never did. In his new job he was scared he would lose it, or wouldn't achieve his ambition of promotion if he were known to be a Christian. He wrote to me to say he hoped I wouldn't be angry, but he would now have to leave Jesus out altogether. I was very sad, but had to respect his choice.

Another girl who became a Christian and really wanted to keep following Jesus had been assigned to teach in a country school. When I visited her she told me she was to marry. At 23 she was expected to marry, and there was only one single young man amongst the teachers at that school, so she had to marry him. The social pressure can be very strong, particularly in the countryside, where traditions die hard. We prayed together that she might keep up her life with Christ despite marrying a non-believer. I have not been able to find out her situation since then.

There are happy stories and sad stories about the work in China as the Gospel seed fell into different kinds of soil. I had never considered myself an evangelist before I went to China, but in the situation it was the most natural thing. When someone asked how they could become a Christian I didn't say "Wait until a pastor comes to pray with you." When they wanted to be baptized I didn't say, "Wait until an ordained minister comes to baptize you" - that might never happen, and I had no compulsion to follow traditions of established denominations. I baptized them, with just a few witnesses, in the nearest river. I sowed the seed and saw some taken away immediately; some flourish for a moment and die; some start to grow but be choked by the pressures of the world; and some begin to bear fruit. The lasting harvest from those few years is in God's hands.

# 16

## AMONGST THE CHINESE IN ENGLAND AND HUNGARY

### England - York

On returning from Hong Kong I settled in York, where I waited for the Lord to show me the next step. Meanwhile I fellowshipped in local churches and worked amongst the Chinese students at the university and in a Bible study group for the Chinese already started by other local Christians. For some time I had a Chinese lodger, Jack. I met him when he was living in another house on my street, but he decided it was more homely in my house, so persuaded me to take him as a lodger. He announced he would call me Mother, and was both a delight and a frustration. He helped in paying the rent, but made the kitchen greasy with his cooking. He had learned the difference between English and Chinese cultures. When I had a new scholar visiting one day, Jack arrived home, greeted the man, took an orange from the fruit bowl and offered it to him. The man refused politely, as was correct, and Jack insisted, until he took it. Taking another orange, Jack offered it to me. I also refused, and this time he put it straight back in the bowl. He knew that a Chinese person must first refuse out of politeness, but an Englishman's "no" is meant. Jack would not have got his M.A. degree without my motherly nagging. I pushed him to retake an exam that was essential to pass, encouraged him to write down the ideas he had in his head for his thesis, and typed it out for him, page by page on the last day. I pushed him out of the door to catch the train to Leeds and hand the finished work in at the very last minute. He passed, and I drove him to Leeds for the degree ceremony. It was a combined effort with a good result. He got his M.A. and I felt like a "Ma". I was sorry to lose touch with him after he returned to China

## Hungary

Sometimes it just says "click" and you know. It was like that when I heard about the many Chinese in Hungary. I don't remember who was the visiting speaker at the Baptist Church in York, or how he came to speak about this. Nor do I remember how I got hold of contacts in Budapest, though it was probably through COCM (Chinese Overseas Christian Mission), with whom I already had some contact. I arranged to go on a visit to Budapest to see for myself the possibilities amongst the Chinese and also in a small English-language Bible Institute recently opened by the pastor of the International Church in Budapest.

My first visit was for a month. All boded well for good co-operation and fruitful ministry on both fronts. During that time I also found a very suitable flat. It had a very large living room, a reasonable bedroom and fairly big kitchen, and was situated in the centre of Pest on a busy tram route, which meant it was easy for folk to find. That was important because my flat became a gathering place for many - Chinese and others. Many complained about the 80 steps up from ground level, but running up and down them several times a day kept me healthy! The small Chinese church there had been started and led by a young Korean pastor. He had been sent out by his church to "be a missionary and plant a church". Unfortunately he was given neither training nor pastoral support in this venture, which made it very hard for him and eventually destroyed both the church and his own personal life. But on my first visit we got on well.

The pastor had to return to Korea for more than half of that first month, so he left me in charge, preaching, counselling, visiting. I got on very well with the Chinese, who appreciated the fact that I had lived in China and knew their language and culture and understood their attitudes much more than Pastor did, as he had neither been to China nor learned the language. (He did learn a little conversational Chinese later.) The church leaders came and told me of their problems with the pastor, things he did that they didn't like. All I could do was advise them to tell him themselves when he came back. They did so, and to him it seemed I had turned the church against him, which made him resent me, though I didn't know this until later.

After a month back in the UK to pack up my belongings I set off again for Hungary. Teamwork was not easy, as I was not familiar with the Korean attitude to pastors - they have a very high standing in society and are very important. I made the mistake of making suggestions which, although he agreed they were good, should have come from him! His problem was that as the younger person he needed to respect me, but as a non-ordained worker and a woman I had to respect him and let him make the suggestions. So we had a slightly uneasy time of working together. He preached through translation. He did speak quite good Hungarian though. I occasionally preached in rather inadequate Chinese, but could converse better. When we had visitors we would take them for a meal to one of the many

Chinese restaurants in the city. The waitresses would speak to him in Chinese and to me in Hungarian, which was obvious from our appearance, but the wrong way round in practice!

Eventually Pastor came to my flat one day and told me he no longer wanted me to work with him in the church. I was kicked out. Because I had no written agreement about the work there was nothing I could do. I found myself able to remain calm, shake his hand and wish him God's blessing, although it did throw me into a very difficult situation. The Chinese were disappointed and some kept in touch. COCM, who were a tower of strength in helping the church, advised me to leave, but I didn't feel God was telling me to do so. I was there to work with the Chinese, with or without a church. I continued attending church for some time, otherwise spending more of my time with the Bible Institute activities, teaching and administrative work. Eventually it became so obvious to the Chinese that the pastor didn't want me there that I felt it best to stay away. A few of them preferred to stay with me and we were able to hold meetings in a small Hungarian Baptist church under the auspices of the International Church. I continued to visit the Chinese, who mostly worked on the extensive Hungarian markets selling Chinese goods, befriended them, witnessed to them, and encouraged them. I was never really happy at that time with the idea of starting a second Chinese church.

A tragic happening during this time brought us briefly together. There was one young Chinese man in the church who was a mature Christian, called Canaan. He was a good help and encouragement in the work. Some time after I had been "excommunicated" by the pastor Canaan wanted to come round and have a chat. I waited for him but he didn't come. Two days later others phoned me to ask if I knew where he was, as he was missing. Eventually they got the police to break into his home, where they found him stabbed to death. The motive could have been money, as some was stolen, but the murderer was never found. I was asked to put up his fiancée and her friend, who came for the funeral from Vienna, where she was studying music. Canaan was sadly missed by all who knew him. This is one of the Lord's ways I will never understand.

Meanwhile I was attending the International Church in Budapest, and sometimes the International Baptist Church, where I found variety and fellowship. I continued teaching at the Bible Institute, with students from Hungary, Romania, Ethiopia and England, which I thoroughly enjoyed. Teaching the Bible in depth was very satisfying, as ministering to the Chinese at that point was on a much simpler level, though I enjoyed that too.

Some Chinese Christians from USA came to take evangelistic meetings and they also reached out to the Chinese in other Hungarian towns. The Korean pastor and I took different towns to follow up. One of the visiting leaders, Thomas Wang of AD2000, tried to mediate between us, but could not persuade Pastor to take me back into the church. Having commuted to my town on a weekly basis for some months I eventually decided to move to my new town, Nyíregyháza, way out east, where I could tend the small flock and work the markets, witnessing to and encouraging the Chinese I found there. Not many responded with faith, though they were friendly enough. It was hard work and showed little fruit. We had regular meetings in a home, and later in rooms hired to us by the local Lutheran church. The first man to become a Christian there was a natural leader and keen to witness where he could. But he told me one day, "It's impossible for the Chinese to get saved." "What about you?" I countered. He didn't have an answer to that. "God can save even the Chinese," I assured him, but he wasn't convinced! I also made Hungarian contacts there and regularly attended the local Baptist church, much appreciating the friendliness of the pastor and his wife. In another town in northern Hungary, Miskolc, there were also a few Chinese on the markets, and I sometimes made a round trip to include them. A few were interested, one young man with slight learning difficulties was really committed to following Jesus, and for some time we had a weekly Bible study there too.

In Budapest I managed best without a car, as parking was a nightmare and public transport was excellent and cheap, but in Nyíregyháza and for the cross-country trips I decided it would be good to have one. I found a red Golf in reasonable condition, and it served me well for several months. When it became evident that I would have to move back to Budapest I began to think about selling it. But when I came out after a half hour visit to hospital it had disappeared. The police were not very helpful, certainly not fast, and I was sure my car was over the border in Romania before they even started looking for it. Many cars were stolen in that area and taken into Romania or Ukraine. This happened in December. With only Third Party insurance I got no compensation. The pastor's wife sympathised - I had kept it in their yard when not using it. "Oh dear," she said. "Now you will have a sad Christmas." "Not at all," I replied. They only took my car. They didn't take my faith, my hope, my joy or my Jesus!!" Although I could have found a good use for the money if I had sold the car, I was determined the thieves should not gain any control over my emotions. Of course I was rather angry at first, but I was happier to be the victim rather than the perpetrator of such a crime.

I made occasional visits to Budapest still and on one such visit met with several of the Chinese Christians I knew. It seemed they had left the church and said many others had too. I suggested I might come back once a month to take a Bible study, so they would have a little spiritual input, but they said no. What they wanted was not a monthly Bible study but a weekly worship service! I swallowed hard, as I realized God was now giving me a challenge that I had been reluctant to face earlier - to plant another Chinese church. I had become friendly with the co-pastor of the Scottish Mission - a cheerful and energetic lady of about my age, and through her I was able to procure the use of the Scottish church, which did not have an evening service -

Chinese services were always in the evening     as most of the people were on the markets all day, even Sundays.

And so began a further six months of commuting between Budapest and Nyíregyháza, a three-hour train journey each way, or a little longer by car. I would stay with a friend in Budapest for two or three days and return home for the rest of the week. Another team from USA came to help us with outreach in Budapest that summer, which swelled our numbers. Soon after this we were able to invite a Taiwanese-American pastor to take over the leadership. He had visited Budapest before so we knew him and appreciated his ministry. My Chinese was still inadequate for regular preaching, and I was very aware of this, though I did my best. The Chinese were very appreciative of my efforts at first, but "familiarity breeds contempt" and as they got to know me they became more demanding, and less satisfied with my level in the language, even though it was improving all the time. Of course they didn't think that if I had used English or Hungarian they would have been completely lost, so Chinese was our only method of communication!

We were a large delegation at the airport to welcome Pastor Chien and his wife and small daughter. At the next Sunday service we officially inducted him and I handed over to him as senior pastor, and said I was happy to be assistant pastor now. But when I asked how we could work together and how I could fit into the work, he turned round and announced that I didn't figure at all in his plans for the church! Talk about having your baby snatched out of your arms.....and then being run over by a steam-roller! This treatment, together with the recent growing criticism of my Chinese, finished me off. I could see no way forwards. I had no self-justification to fall back on. The church was God's, not mine, and a Chinese person could serve it better than I could - that was why I had handed over the senior position to him. And of course I was aware of my limited Chinese, even if I was managing fairly well with it. But still.... the treatment I received was too harsh. I escaped to Finland on a two-week ticket. My Mission Director met me, to make sure I hadn't had a complete breakdown, and put me on the train to the countryside.

There in Finland I was able to feel wanted again. I could walk in the forest or by the seaside and commune with the Lord in the silence. It was quietness I needed after the harsh words of rejection. There was one spot in the forest where I would stop and look up at the tops of the surrounding trees. I gave each treetop a name - grace, love, mercy, peace, patience, goodness, glory, etc. and revelled in the feeling of being surrounded by all these qualities of my Lord. Concerned friends, who had also been through a trauma, came to visit and encourage me. And after the two weeks I was restored and on my feet again. The devil had kicked hard, but he was not to have the victory!

Being restored in Finland is one thing; going back to Hungary, to the situation that had hit me so hard was another. But I believe the Lord had been working there too. Pastor Chien accepted me as a co-worker (in his slightly macho way) and I heard no more critical voices about my Chinese. In fact, the work developed well, many Chinese were saved and taught. We had regular baptisms as one by one they rejected their background of communism, buddhism or self-reliance, and gave their lives to Jesus. There were usually ten to 20 candidates at each baptism, usually about equal number of men and women. Pastor would baptize the men and I the women. Christians who are familiar only with the tradition of only priests/pastors baptizing have wondered at this. However there is no teaching in the Bible to support that tradition. Baptismal teaching was given, and then teaching courses were held by mature Christians on Knowing God and on the practical Christian life.

After the first year we heard that the Korean pastor had finally left the country for good. He had left once before, more than a year earlier, and I had been invited back into the church at that time. But to the disappointment of many he reappeared and took over again, this time freezing me out by refusing to even look at me or speak to me. But now he really had gone. The remaining few from his church disowned the previous name because of its connections and tried to carry on under a new name and with a new venue. A visiting preacher suggested we join forces and form one church again. We agreed on this - using their venue and our pastor. But first there was some work to be done on forgiveness and reconciliation to heal the resentment, guilt or bitterness that had been felt by various individuals. A meeting was arranged for this purpose. It was good to see people going up to each other to say sorry, and a handshake or hug showed they had been forgiven. I was touched when Pastor came to me and prayed for me in a way that approached an apology. This new arrangement worked well. Pastor Chien, his wife and I were the pastoral team, and deacons were chosen for various responsibilities such as leading the service and teaching the adult Sunday School which always preceded the service.

One particular joy was to see a group of 12 come from Nyíregyháza to be baptized. Yes, there were the people I had witnessed to, discussed with, shared God's love with. It had taken time for them to respond, but as others continued the work I had started, now the fruit had ripened. I smiled at the brother who had said the Chinese couldn't be saved. "You see, God is able", and this time he was very happy to agree with me!

After the six months of commuting from Nyíregyháza to Budapest, completing my year in Nyíregyháza, I moved back to Budapest, to my old flat, which happened to be free again. My landlord had had bad tenants after I left and was happy to have me back, even agreeing to keep the rent at the previous level for some time! Christians from the Budapest church took turns in travelling to Nyíregyháza to continue the work. Meanwhile, my flat continued to be a venue for some English classes, for church council meetings and for fellowship and personal counselling. I recall the wife of a Christian man coming to me one day. He had been the first to be baptized, but she was back in China and their marriage was very shaky. I encouraged him to invite her to join him in Budapest. When she came she had little interest in the Gospel and only came to church because he persuaded her. Being an intelligent woman she decided to find out what it was all about, and came several times to study the Bible in my home. I gave her time and space to make her own decision. Then came the day when she arrived saying now she wanted to accept Jesus as her Saviour. I was overjoyed, and she was the last person I baptized. It was good to see this couple developing from contemplating divorce, through faith in Jesus to serving the Lord together. I also continued to arrange parties where my Chinese friends could meet people from other countries. Over a period of time we had Christians from USA, Scotland, Germany, Sudan, Romania and Hungary.

## Vivien

At the end of my first spell in Budapest I was able to make contact with my Chinese "daughter" Vivien again. After some faxed correspondence I invited her to Hungary for three months to visit me. I would care for her needs here if she could pay her fare. She could, and it was a wonderful moment when we met again after five years. I wanted her to get some good Bible teaching at the Bible Institute. By the time she came I had moved out east, so she lived with other students in a Christian family and visited me whenever she could. After three months she felt she had only just got started, and wanted to finish the year. I was using my small income to pay for her board and lodging and pocket money, but we managed. (The fall in value of the Hungarian forint against sterling, which was the currency I received my support in, meant the money went a little further each month, despite rising prices. So this was the best time to have those extra expenses of supporting two.) After that year she wanted to complete the course by doing the second year. By then

I was moving back to Budapest and she came to stay with me. I said that as long as the Lord provided me with the means I would continue to support her. She was appreciated at the Bible Institute for her joy and her fighting spirit - theological English was a real challenge for her - and in the Chinese church for her brightness and loving attitude. We made a couple of visits to Prague together to minister to the small Chinese Church there. During our second visit they invited her to move there and pastor their fellowship after she had graduated. We felt this was of the Lord. Graduation was a happy day, and soon after Vivien was farewelled by the Budapest church, as she was going as their missionary. Then we travelled up to Prague, where she was inducted into her new ministry. For me it was a time of remembering and rejoicing - this firstfruit of that desperately hard first year in China, now trained and able to minister to her own people. In the weeks and months after her conversion I had seen the potential of a Bible teacher in her, as she helped me to evangelise both amongst the students and amongst her own relatives. And now to see her in that role, despite the earlier official ban on our correspondence, showed that the Lord is not bound by any ban. He was working in her during those quiet years, teaching her to overcome the many frustrations she met, maturing her as a person and preparing her for the job of leading others to faith in Him and maturing them in their faith. God knows what He is doing all the time. Vivien is now back in China, married, and serving the Lord through her local church. We don't know what the future holds for her and her husband.

When I reached the British retiring age of 60 I felt I needed a break, not to retire, but to "re-tyre" and prepare for further service. I decided to take a sabbatical year in Finland, renew closer contact with my home church in Helsinki, and take a rest from the stresses of Chinese ministry. It meant I could be within fairly easy reach of Helsinki and could visit my home church there more often, renewing close ties with folk there. I don't know what I had expected of a sabbatical year, but with hindsight would have arranged it differently, giving myself chance for further studies, for example. But the Lord helped me through the frustrations and difficulties I encountered, and it was good to have a rest from my previous work.

# 17

## BACK HOME IN MANCHESTER

My first contacts with Chinese work in Britain came during my year and a half in York after returning from China. Through contacts there I was taken along to meetings of a group called China Action Group (CAG). This was an informal gathering of people from different missions who worked amongst the Chinese in Britain. I was soon asked to act as secretary for our gatherings and became aware of the scope of the work. One couple, Douglas and Rosie Sadler from Manchester, were working amongst the academic Mainland Chinese students there. I met them again some years later, during my last year in Hungary. They felt I might be a help to their work, as I spoke more Chinese than they did. The invitation was given to come to Manchester, but I had already made the decision to take a sabbatical year in Finland, and at best could only put the idea on hold.

As my sabbatical year in Finland was drawing to a close the question of the next step had to be considered. The invitation to work in Manchester was still there, and I made a visit in late spring to get to know the people and the situation. I got involved in the activities of the church for two weeks - teaching a small group in their English teaching club known as English Corner, attending the Sunday Fellowship, and meeting individuals. Our last activity was a day outing to Llangollen in the minibus. I was to stay there with friends for a few days. As we said goodbye, standing amongst the beautiful Welsh mountains, some of them said "See you again soon." "Maybe" was my uncertain answer. Douglas said he thought he wouldn't see me again.

But back in Finland, as I kept the matter before the Lord in prayer, He was ready with the answer. My daily Bible reading happened to be taking me through Genesis at the time, and came one day to chapter 31, part of the story of Jacob. In verse three the Lord said to Jacob: "Go back to the land of your fathers and to your relatives, and I will be with you." It was so clear at that moment that the words were for me. The land of my fathers, yes, even the city where I had grown up, and my relatives, yes, my sister was living in the Greater Manchester area. And having lived away from the UK for almost all of 35 years I was not sure if I could fit in again, so I needed that final phrase "and I will be with you." I informed the Sadlers of my decision, to their great delight. I would come, I said, for the four years up to my official Finnish retirement.

But then something funny happened. We were holding tent meetings in the place where I was staying in Finland, and whilst evenings were more evangelistic the morning sessions were for believers. One morning the speaker came in and said, "I am going to talk about prophecy today. How the Lord might use you to say to somebody, for example, 'The Lord is sending you to China and you will get confirmation in three weeks." It wasn't a prophecy, merely an example, but my heart jumped. I knew it was for me, but couldn't understand it. "Lord," I objected, "You have just told me I am to go to Britain, so how can you send me to China?" Taking comfort from the promise of confirmation in three weeks I put it from my mind. But just three days later I received an e-mail from an American acquaintance in Hungary. This older lady explained that she had a Chinese "daughter" who was now back in Shanghai and dying. She would love to visit her, but had never been to China and spoke no Chinese. Would I go with her if she paid my ticket? We would go for about a week. Now the non-prophecy fell into place - it wasn't long-term, only a very short refresher for me before re-starting work amongst the Chinese. I was able to postpone my move to Britain by two weeks, so that apart from the Chinese week I could have a few days renewing contact with friends in Budapest.

We flew via Paris, where we had a long wait - just at the precise time of the total eclipse of the sun. Dark glasses were handed out and we all watched it getting darker. Unfortunately, just for the couple of minutes of the total eclipse a small cloud drifted into just the wrong place, so annoying! One small boy opposite was looking through his dark glasses, then took them off and looked at the darkening sun. Turning to his daddy he announced with delight, "Daddy, I can see the sun without the glasses!" Daddy reacted fast and the dark glasses were soon back on!

The week in Shanghai was sad in that we made daily visits to the lady who was dying with a brain tumour, and suffering very frequent spasms. But she was so happy to see us, and thrilled when I read the Bible to her in Chinese and sang some Chinese songs. "Oh, sing it again," she said, "I want to join in." I hadn't known that she was a keen singer herself. The family was also very grateful to us for coming, and looked after us very well, taking us sightseeing when we were not at the hospital. We visited a "water village" which was a miniature Venice, and were taken another day to a large food court. Stalls filled the hall and all kinds of food were served. We decided to try western food - Chinese style. This involved the difficult task of eating a delicious Wiener schnitzel with chopsticks! (Well, you eat Chinese food with a knife and fork in Britain, don't you? That is just as ridiculous!) For me it was good to be able to help my friend as interpreter and companion, and to minister to a dying sister, and be a blessing to her family. It was also interesting to visit Shanghai, to see the old and the new side by side - backyard vegetable markets like I knew from my years further south, and the amazingly imaginative architecture of the new skyscrapers and other public buildings. Previously Chinese friends had been horrified to hear I had lived in China but never visited Beijing or Shanghai. Now I had redeemed that situation at least in part. And it was God's gift to me to restart my Chinese ministry with a refresher course on what China is like today.

On returning to Finland I was ready to dispatch my boxes of belongings and fly to Manchester. As my sister had a family living with her there was no room for me, so she found me a room in a student house owned by her church. So again I was virtually homeless for two months, first a couple of weeks in the student room and then in the Sadlers' house as they went abroad for a month. My boxes had arrived from Finland and even though I had to stay on for a while after their return, my hosts kindly managed to cope with me and a lounge full of boxes. Finding what I needed from the boxes, despite a reasonable degree of organisation in the packing, was like playing a game of Memory - now which box did I see that in last time I was digging around?? It was a bigger version of living in a suitcase, and it had its frustrations, and was harder to cope with than when I was younger, but I saw it as part of my maxi-risk life and the Lord helped me through the two months of homelessness. Meanwhile I was looking for a house or flat. In my ignorance I had supposed you find a place, pay the money and move in! But no, there were weeks of surveys, solicitor's searches etc, so it was not until the middle of November that I could move into my own little flat, - the first time I had actually owned the place I lived in. It felt unfamiliar but good. I was able to collect my stored furniture from the church attic in York, where it had been gathering dust for some years, and began to settle in. There was much to learn, and asking "stupid" questions in a Manchester dialect brought some strange looks! This was culture shock in reverse (also known as re-entry shock) and it is harder than going to a foreign country where you expect to find things strange. Yes, even moving back to Britain was a risky business situation in a different way. Being a "foreigner" in your own country feels awkward, but then it is all part of the cost of following Jesus wherever he leads. The parts of central Manchester I had known as a child were barely recognizable, though driving round Sale, where we had actually lived, brought back many memories. But the past is the past and I like to live in the present. It has been good to get to know my younger sister better as an adult, though we had kept in fairly good touch through the years and she had visited me abroad several times.

The Chinese work in Manchester was in many ways very different from the work in Hungary. There the Chinese were uneducated people (mostly), who knew how to do business. Here in Manchester they are mainly academics, working for a Masters degree or a Ph.D, or doing post-doctorate research etc., much more sophisticated, and always very busy. More recently the numbers of undergraduates and asylum seekers have increased. Our Sunday Fellowship is small but growing. At first I was asked to sometimes preach or lead the meetings, but gradually we have trained the Chinese themselves to do the leading and God has sent us able Chinese preachers. The problem in training leaders is that people come and go. After their degree or study course they often move on to other cities or other countries, some returning to China. So our Fellowship is more of a channel than a pool, and we trust that the things they have learnt in Manchester will be lived out in whatever city or country they now live in. Apart from the long-term students there are also visiting scholars staying for short periods. Our aim is to reach them with the Gospel even in a short stay, and for long-term students train them in the ways of the Lord, though it is frustrating when they then move away and we need to train new people.

To get initial contact we have our English club, known according to Chinese tradition as English Corner. Many newly arrived Chinese find their way there to improve their English, including families of students. Although we can talk about any subject - culture, language, geography, grammar, I have often had openings to talk about the Bible and Jesus. Sometimes the students bring up the subject, sometimes it comes in a natural way into the conversation. Most start with an academic interest, which may then become a spiritual interest. I find it both exciting and challenging to explain the Gospel to somebody who knows absolutely nothing about it, or has heard only a few stories, especially as they are often so open to listen to explanations about Jesus and the Bible. You don't find many British people with either this level of ignorance (though I'm sure there are many nowadays) or this level of openness. Home Bible studies with a group, or with individual wives of students were also part of my work, and explaining the Christian life more deeply was also a joy and a challenge, because the Chinese traditions do not incorporate Christian principles or even references to Bible stories or characters, as do those of western countries.

One visiting doctor who came to our Friday Bible study group told us that his wife was a Christian, but didn't know much about Jesus. Apparently she had been led to faith by an old lady, who had later moved away, and contact had been lost. Such a tentative believer did not have the boldness to go to church and ask more about Jesus. So her husband was keen to come to our group and learn what he could. We overheard him on the phone once, telling a friend he was thinking of becoming a Christian. After about eight weeks he took the step of inviting Jesus into his life, which left him just a month to learn about the faith from inside. As he left he announced, "Now I am going home to teach my wife about the Jesus she believes in!"

It has been said that a missionary's work is to work him/herself out of a job. At the end of the promised four years I feel this has been achieved and so I could happily retire from this work. The work was not easy, though often full of joy and satisfaction, and I feel it is right to leave it behind me and move again into the unknown.

# CONCLUSION & REFLECTIONS

In these chapters I have told of the personality and gifts that God gave me as He "knit me together in my mother's womb" (Ps.139v13). We are given different gifts and different personalities. God can use them all, all that is, that are offered back to Him. Using them for myself, I could have been a pretty awful person. Using our talents for God comes from a biblical story, as you probably remember. The man with only one talent hid it in the ground and didn't use it. His master was angry with him. Yet many people speak of envying my talents. "If only I could communicate like you, sing like you, etc." That is not what God wants us to do. Even with only one talent we are expected to use it. No servant in the story was left without a talent, and neither are we. Talents vary and needs vary. There are many things I cannot do, which others can. We need to bring our talents together and use them to build up God's Kingdom. Everyone is needed. And the Bible also says that of him to whom much has been given, much will be required. I have been given much, many talents, and God has led me into situations where I could use them for His glory.

I put my life into God's hand and became a missionary. Others have done the same and been led into secular careers. God has a plan for each one of us if we will put our lives fully into His hand.

I put my life into God's hand and am not married. (For me as a Christian this naturally means no sexual experiences.) Others have done the same and are happily married. But sadly, I know many Christians who have not asked the Lord about this matter and have made their own choice, usually with the result that they could not serve the Lord as they wanted, sometimes with the result that they themselves have backslidden in their relationship with Jesus.

I put my life into God's hand and have had to live on very little money. Others have done the same and had an easier lifestyle, but also been able to give more to God's work. He only asks that we be faithful with what we have and He will see it is enough. Through giving tithes and offerings to the Lord He has kept me like the "princess" I am.

We need always to be ready to go into a challenging situation without thinking about our own self-betterment or the fulfilment of a dream. And even at home we can "walk the walk" so our family, neighbours, colleagues, can see Jesus in us. And then we should be willing to "talk the talk" when God gives us the opportunity? It all needs a lot of courage, but that is what the Holy Spirit wants to give us when we let Him.

You maybe have seen throughout this book why the Lord gave me a strong will and pioneer spirit. I certainly needed it in this work of travelling in many countries and learning many new languages. Most people are happier in teamwork than out on their own, and that is quite all right. But even as a pioneer I have had to work in a team sometimes. "Realizing your potential" is good when it is done for God, but it has its limits, and should not be used in the modern selfish sense of the expression. The "stickability" was something I had to learn - that is part of character-building. It is sometimes difficult to move at God's pace and not our own, but it is best to keep in step with Him.

Nowadays you can take Bibles into Eastern Europe without problem, but there are many kinds of adventure still awaiting those who have the desire to follow Jesus whatever the cost. It may not be travelling, but then again it may. It may not be to any of the countries I went to, but there are many other countries that are a challenge for the Christian living a maxi-risk life.

We have a great God, a God we can trust, a God who is faithful and compassionate. It was perhaps with only a little knowledge of this God that I set out to follow Him with all my heart. Through the years I have learned more of His greatness, His faithfulness, and His mercy towards my failings and mistakes. It is His grace that has brought me safe thus far, and as the song says, it is grace that will lead me home.

When I look back on my life this far I can only praise Him for His generosity and grace towards me. Through all the difficulties I have learned to know my Lord better. With an easier life I might not have been so dependent on Him, so I can praise for the hard times too. I have been sad, weak, fearful and depressed at times, but also rejoiced in my salvation, in the beauty of God's world, in the kindness of friends, in warm fellowship in many countries, in the many different experiences, in the fun I have had, and in the joy of sharing my Lord and His Word with others.

I would like to encourage you, my reader, to get to know God better through following Him with your whole heart, and with all the talents He has given you, be they many or few. This book is a testimony to God's greatness, but He has no favourites, and will be for you the same wonderful Father and Lord He has been for me. I give Him the glory for the good deeds He had prepared for me, and that He led me to walk in. He has good deeds prepared for you too. I pray this book may be an inspiration and help for somebody, maybe just for you.

Retirement doesn't mean being inactive, as many active Christian pensioners prove.

To the extent that my health and strength allow with advancing years I hope to continue to serve Him. At present I am "re-tyred" and looking forwards rather than backwards. Since summer 2005, when I went with an ECM team to Former East Germany, I have been making regular visits to a small church near Leipzig, where I have done preaching, home visiting, English teaching (to attract new people to the church) and run a mini-bible school. The church has limited personnel resources and is glad to have this extra resource to help the many new Christians their witness has won. We aim to continue these visits, and I am also open for other opportunities, whether in English or another language. Only God knows what the future holds, and still in Maxi-risk mode, I still long to serve Him with all my strength and mind and soul.

I am ready to travel, speak, witness, teach, or write, serving God through serving people. I can be contacted by e-mail: pauline@stableford.fslife.co.uk